# Instructional Design for Teac

"This book is a treasure for teachers! First, it is highly reader-friendly. It uses plain, engaging language, accompanied by helpful visuals, examples, and stories. And it is organized for easy access, such as having call-out boxes for heuristics and common errors. Second, this book presents powerful ideas for improving student learning, both in terms of the teacher's planning process and the teaching methods that are most likely to help students learn. Third, this book is flexible. It offers variations for different approaches to teaching, such as behaviorist, constructivist, user-design, inquiry learning, and standards-based curriculum. I strongly recommend this book for teachers at all levels of education."

*Charles Reigeluth, Professor, Instructional Systems Technology, Indiana University, Bloomington, USA*

"I am delighted with the information in this text! It breaks down the ID process in a very sensible and teacher-friendly manner. Standards-based learning has created an atmosphere wherein the lesson planning process feels very much out of teachers' hands. This text shows teachers how to take back the reins of their lesson planning—how to creatively analyze, synthesize, and implement their own well-thought-out goals, objectives, and individual lessons. In short, the text teaches teachers a shorthand process for creating sensible lessons that originate from the standards but grow out of their own identities as teachers. For this, I say, 'Well done!'"

*Melissa Merritt, 17-year Veteran Home School Teacher/ Middle School Teacher, Fort Collins, Colorado, USA*

"This book is an invaluable tool for teachers who want to plan interesting and effective lessons for their students. It not only provides teachers with a very practical, easy-to-employ model for designing instruction, it also demonstrates how the model can be integrated with a wide variety of teaching approaches that are popular today, ranging from constructivist, student-centered techniques to standards-based instructional methods. If you are a pre-service or in-service teacher who wants to improve instruction and learning in your classroom, you should definitely read this book!"

*Robert A. Reiser, Distinguished University Teaching Professor and Robert M. Morgan Professor of Instructional Systems, Florida State University, USA*

"*Instructional Design for Teachers* is a very teacher-friendly and easy-to-read book full of great ideas for both the first-year and veteran teachers among us who are interested in using instructional design tomorrow in our classrooms. This book takes you step by step through the processes of implementation on a very practical and delightful journey. If you want to be a better teacher, read *Instructional Design for Teachers.*"

*Kitsy Fisher, 31-year Kindergarten Teacher, Dublin, Ohio, USA*

*Instructional Design for Teachers, Second Edition* focuses on the instructional design (ID) process specifically for K-12 teachers. The first edition introduced a new, common-sense model of instructional design to take K-12 teachers through the ID process step by step, with a special emphasis on preparing, motivating, and encouraging new and ongoing use of ID principles. This second edition includes new material on design in gaming, cybercharters, online classrooms, and flipped classrooms, as well as special considerations for the Common Core.

Each chapter contains framing questions, common errors, easy-to-use rules of thumb, clearly stated outcomes, and examples showing ID in action. The basic model and its application within constructivism and user-design will help teachers adapt from a behavioral approach to a more open, student-centered design approach. Combining basics with strategies to implement this model in the most advanced instructional approaches, this book empowers teachers and learners to use good instructional design with the most recent research-based approaches to learning.

*Instructional Design for Teachers* shows how ID principles can impact instructional moments in positive and practical ways. The book can be used for basic ID courses and introductory curriculum courses, and is accessible to in-service as well as pre-service teachers.

**Alison A. Carr-Chellman,** PhD, is Department Head of Learning and Performance Systems and Professor of Education (Learning, Design, and Technology) at Pennsylvania State University, USA.

# Instructional Design for Teachers

Improving Classroom Practice

Second Edition

**Alison A. Carr-Chellman**

Routledge
Taylor & Francis Group

NEW YORK AND LONDON

Second edition published 2016
by Routledge
711 Third Avenue, New York, NY 10017

and by Routledge
2 Park Square, Milton Park, Abingdon, Oxon OX14 4RN

*Routledge is an imprint of the Taylor & Francis Group, an informa business*

© 2016 Taylor & Francis

The right of Alison A. Carr-Chellman to be identified as the author of this work has been asserted by her in accordance with sections 77 and 78 of the Copyright, Designs and Patents Act 1988.

First published by Routledge 2011

*Library of Congress Cataloging in Publication Data*
Carr-Chellman, Alison A.
  Instructional design for teachers : improving classroom practice /
  Alison A. Carr-Chellman.—Second edition.
    pages cm
  Includes bibliographical references and index.
  1. Instructional systems—Design.   2. Computer-assisted instruction.
  3. Curriculum planning.   4. Educational technology.   I. Title.
  LB1028.38.C36 2015
  371.3—dc23                                    2014045440

ISBN: 978-1-138-77680-7 (hbk)
ISBN: 978-1-138-77681-4 (pbk)
ISBN: 978-1-315-77303-2 (ebk)

Typeset in Caslon
by RefineCatch Limited, Bungay, Suffolk

Printed and bound in the United States of America by Publishers Graphics, LLC on sustainably sourced paper.

To my mother, Patricia Burns Carr 1931–2013, my inspiration for teaching and for tilting at educational reform windmills. We did it Mama and I'm still thinking BIG!

# Contents

# Figures and Tables

## Figures

## Tables

# Foreword

When you purchase a new desk at Wally World, it is never assembled. It is always in a box with the picture on the outside. It is up to you to assemble it, that is, put the pieces together in such a way as to make them resemble the picture on the outside. In many ways, teaching can be viewed as similar to putting together the new desk. We often start with a pretty good picture of what it is that we want our students to learn, and we know all of the various components that go into the learning process like texts, media, tests, and of course, the learners themselves. The problem becomes how we integrate all of the pieces in such a way that they match that outcome we had in mind when we started.

To stay with our analogy, perhaps the most important thing in that box with all the pieces of our new desk is the directions. Without them, we can use our intuitions and prior experiences to try to figure out how to put the various pieces together, but we may find that some things just don't seem to fit anywhere, and some things seem to be backwards. There is a lot of trial and error, and we may never get the desk to look like the picture on the box. However, if we are provided with well-organized, step-by-step directions for integrating the pieces in the box, hopefully with illustrations to guide us, we have a pretty good chance of being successful in assembling the desk.

In our analogy, the key component is the directions for assembling the desk. Instructional design can serve the same function for teachers who want to integrate the resources at their disposal to facilitate students' acquisition of the goals for their instruction. Instructional design is a process, or series of suggested steps, that teachers can use to plan, implement, and evaluate their instruction. In the same way that directions are useful for helping us assemble a desk, instructional design can help us use what is available to us to help students achieve the desired learning outcomes (just like the picture on the outside of the box that the pieces of the desk came in).

Instructional design has evolved as a process over a number of years. It was originally developed as a tool for designing, implementing and evaluating corporate and military training, and it has been used very successfully to do so. In more recent years, there have been significant efforts to find ways to apply the instructional design process to public education. You have, in this book, a demonstration of the fundamental concepts of instructional design presented in the context of the realities of the public school classroom.

In this text you will learn about the basic instructional design process that includes the setting of goals, establishing learner objectives, identifying critical learner characteristics and abilities, developing or selecting appropriate tests, selecting texts and media, and implementing, evaluating and revising your instruction. Most importantly, you will come to recognize the importance of aligning these components so that the end result is effective and efficient instruction. Awareness of the need for alignment will be one of the most important outcomes of using this book.

A second feature of this text is the inclusion of a number of different approaches that are currently in use in classrooms. In other words, the use of instructional design does not pre-suppose that you are in a traditional classroom, but you may be. You may be using a required curriculum or a set of standards required by your state or No Child Left Behind. You may prefer to use inquiry learning or user-design approaches to your teaching. You will find examples here of how you can integrate the instructional design process into the planning and implementation of these various approaches.

You may have heard about instructional design and have been concerned that it just takes too much time to do all the planning that seems to be required by this approach. There is no denying that it does take time to use it the first time, then a little less the second, and then less and less as you master the process. Think back to our analogy about the use of directions to build our desk. Consider how much faster you could build a second desk, and then the next and the next. It is not a perfect analogy because some of the pieces change each time we plan a new lesson, but not all of them.

The "inventors" of the instructional design process, who were learning psychologists, wanted to create a process that went well beyond the creation of instruction that focused on the learners' acquisition of knowledge. We know that we can use simple drills on computers to facilitate the memorization of facts and information. The emphasis in the instructional design process is not only to identify the knowledge that students must have, but also the skills and attitudes that will lead to their future success in the classroom and in the real world. Good luck in your mastery of this powerful planning and teaching tool.

**Walter Dick**
*Huntsville, Alabama*
*February 2010*

# Acknowledgments

Thank you so much to Susan Farber and Bridget Fox for the first round of teacher-informed reviews, Kitsy Fisher, Missy Merritt, and Lyssa Fisher-Rogers for the second round of teacher-informed reviews.

Thank you to Brendan Bagley, Jonathan Michael, Jennifer Landry, Bridget Fox, and Caitlin Conroy for agreeing to contribute examples and samples from their own classroom practice to this book project.

Thank you also to Kimbr Filko for her excellent work on the graphics throughout this book.

I am also indebted to Dr. Walter Dick for providing the Foreword to this work. He has been an inspiration to generations of instructional designers and I deeply appreciate his reflections on this work

**In Memoriam**
"If your students don't leave your class at least once a semester with a headache, you're not doing your job."

*David Jonassen*

# 1

# WHAT IS INSTRUCTIONAL DESIGN?

**Chapter Questions**

1. What is instructional design for teachers?
2. Why do we call this a systems approach?
3. What are some of the benefits of using ID in the classroom?
4. What are some of the drawbacks of using ID in the classroom?
5. What are two things you can do to use this book optimally?

## What Is Instructional Design for the Classroom?

*It's Common Sense!*

First, let me assure you, instructional design (or ID as we fondly call it) is not rocket science. Sometimes it may feel as if it is much harder than rocket science, but ID is really fairly straightforward and I'll bet you will find it feels pretty intuitive—it's very much applied common sense. As you work through the content of this book, you may feel that you already know these basic ideas, or that you learned it a slightly different way earlier in your teaching career or in an earlier course. You may even find that this all makes sense and it's how you've been creating learning and instruction in your classroom for years. Even if you've never set foot in a classroom, this book will help you to see how ID can improve learning moments in any classroom. This is a promise I can make with 20 years of experience designing learning in classrooms for K-12, higher education, and even corporate settings. I've created learning in tutoring centers for 4-year-olds, and in Navy pilot training centers for advanced air combat maneuvering. I've created classroom instruction at the elementary and secondary levels, as well as many years of courses for both online and face-to-face college courses. I've had a lot of chances to get this right, and plenty of screw-ups too and

I've seen that there are a few things that if we can simply understand and apply them well, *will* make my classroom, and I'm confident, your classroom, work better at the job of true learning.

So although ID is a pretty simple set of skills that you can exercise daily, it can be frustrating as well. ID is a very disciplined approach to designing learning situations in your classroom. It may seem silly at some level as you go through the steps. Avoid the tendency to say, "Oh I know how to do that already, I'll skip to the really difficult stuff." Please take one step at a time and stay in that step, stay in that moment of instructional design for as long as it takes you to really understand what is needed to create a good goal statement, well-written objectives, or properly integrated technology decisions. Don't rush through the process. In this way, this skinny little book may be a bit deceiving because in order to really effectively use these ideas in your classroom, you have to internalize them, to bring them into your thinking in a fresh way. That will require time spent really thinking about these steps and ideas, and digesting them. You will need to make the translation into your own unique classroom experience so that you will see ways that you can easily, seamlessly implement these ideas. I'm going to help you with that a great deal, but sitting and thinking about these ideas will be critical for your ability to transform what may seem at first to be a clunky or difficult or overly long process into a set of heuristics, or brief rules of thumb, that you will fall back on every day. Heuristics are guides that can be easily and quickly called upon to help you find the best solution. They are a way to help you use the model in a more intuitive and comfortable way.

As you can tell, I believe that there are some really important gifts that ID can offer to a classroom. While separately the steps may seem familiar, even simplistic, as a system, working together and carefully interwoven, it is probably going to be a new experience for you to see the ways that we make sure tests, for example, align with the content, goals, and classroom activities. ID can help you focus your instruction so that you are really reaching the learning goals you have for your students. It helps you to concentrate your efforts toward specific learning goals that are then *supported* by appropriate objectives, tests, integrated technology, and classroom activities.

## Simple Definition

The definition of instructional design for teachers is simply the process by which instruction is created for classroom use through a systematic process of setting goals, creating learning objectives, analyzing student characteristics, writing tests, selecting materials, developing activities, selecting media, implementing and revising the lesson. Each of these steps will be discussed in complete detail in this book, starting in Chapter 2 with examples of how teachers can and have used these steps to create effective lessons in their classrooms every day.

### *Steps in the ID Process*

The field of ID has been around for a long time. Coming from the use of audio visuals in military applications to ensure that large numbers of soldiers are up and running as quickly as possible, the field has worked through the past decades to clarify and research the best way to create good learning experiences and environments. The basic steps in this model for the general ID professional are:

1. Analyze needs.
2. Design instruction.
3. Develop materials.
4. Implement the instruction.
5. Evaluate and revise the instruction.

Most in the field know this as the ADDIE model, based on the first letters in each step. For the purposes of learning about ID in the classroom, we're going to dispense with the use of step 1 for the most part. We will analyze our learners, and our context, but we aren't really going to look at needs. This is, in general, because within the classroom, there are requirements and those needs are often determined at a much higher, even a community or political, level. We all realize that there are some standards, for example, that we don't necessarily think make sense for a given developmental level, but they're there, and pretty immutable. So we dispense with the long and arduous task of doing a full-needs assessment in which we would determine whether the need was really instructional, and so forth. Instead we will focus our efforts on a recasting of the remaining four steps into a nine-step model as outlined in Chapter 2.

*Principles of ID*

These are some good points to remember when you're doing instructional design on your own.

1. *Know where you're going* There's a saying—perhaps from Native American originally, but applied from Mager's work (1975) on instructional objectives—which says something like, "Knowing where you are is a function of knowing where you've come from and where you're going." My own children have a framed calligraphy of a saying from my husband's family, "Remember who you are and where you come from." While they may sound trite, these are important foundations for good instruction. You need to have clear goals and objectives for your learners. They should be defined in such a way that you know (and so does your learner) when they've reached that goal. So it is important that you clearly understand and clearly state your goal.

2. *Know your learners* It is essential that you understand who your learners are, what motivates them, why they are reluctant to learn, which ones will embrace an idea, and which ones need more relevance, for example. The process of analyzing your student characteristics will be the main place where you can focus on knowing your learners with relation to the specific content for the instruction.

3. *Be creative with your activities and media* It is important to remember that novelty is a good motivator even though we don't want to select expensive media *just* to motivate. Doing creative things with your classroom instruction will produce better results overall. Avoid ruts and comfort and keep reaching for the stars, doing new things, creating exciting and fun approaches to your classroom-learning experiences.

4. *Do drafts and iterate!* You'll find that ID is a process of iteration. Like good writing, it is imperative that you revisit earlier decisions and plan to make changes as new things emerge in the process of instructional design. Don't create documents and set

them into stone with the expectation that they will never change. That is antithetical to the whole point of ID, which is a flexible and open process.

5. *Test out your instruction and materials with a similar population and revise* Make sure that you are able to try out your instruction with a population that is as similar to your target population as possible. Take the results and feedback they're able to give you and change the materials and instructional approach if necessary to better meet the needs of your learners.

6. *Align, align, align* As they say in real estate, it's all about location, right? Here in instructional design it's all about alignment. The goals should be aligned with the objectives, which should be aligned with the test items, and the media and activities, and so forth. What does this alignment mean? It means that you're not testing on something that you think is important but that isn't represented in your objectives—a surprise then to the learner. It means that you select activities and media that support reaching your goals and objectives rather than selecting activities that are fun or comfortable, but don't support the learning. Alignment is perhaps the most important piece of advice I can give you in terms of good instructional design.

7. *Do ID all the time* Instructional design should fit nicely into your life as a classroom teacher. It does not have to be something that you only do when you have great amounts of time to devote to it. Yes, you may find it appropriate to pay particular attention to the practice of ID when you're planning your classes in the summer before the first day of school. But you may also find it seeping into your every moment throughout every day. It's best not to sequester ID into only large planning time blocks, particularly as those may come all too rarely! Consider ID as a process you can use all the time.

*The Systems Puzzle*

The idea that this is a *systemic* process is an important one, and there are some distinctions I'd like to make here in regard to systems approaches. To begin, an easy way to understand a system is as any combination of elements that work together. In its simplest conception, a system could be a motorcycle, a clock, or a human body. These are mechanical systems that work in very predictable ways. Generally speaking, if a part of a mechanical system is broken, we can take that part out, repair it, reinsert it into the system, and voilà! The system will work again. But we also understand there are many more complex systems that aren't mechanical, such as organizations, classrooms, and families. These are much more difficult to repair when they're not working properly. Thus, if a family member is ill, if you remove the family member, and send them to rehabilitation (for drug use, for example) and reinsert them into the family, they'll rarely "fix" the problem in the family and far too often revert to their old ways precisely *because* they are embedded in a familial context that was already ill with addiction. Social systems like these, as with instructional moments in classrooms, are truly complex systems. This means that we can understand systems as pieces that are contextualized and working together. In the case of instruction in classrooms, what follows then is that when we understand our learning goal, that goal *drives* the potential solutions that we might consider for the activities and technology to be integrated into that lesson.

This is a very precise procedure, in part because we are working systemically, where all the pieces fit together like a jigsaw puzzle, but a puzzle with slightly flexible pieces. Because precision is not demanded up front in order to create the solution, this allows for some level of errors that you may not see or understand until you realize that the instruction isn't working, but you may not be sure why. When fixing a clock, if a piece isn't milled properly, it simply will not fit, and you have to go back and retool it until it does fit. But instruction doesn't work like that, so a part can be put into place (improperly formed objectives, for example, or test items that are not reflective of the learning goals) and you may not realize it until months later when something seems to be wrong and not working with the learning environment.

Figuring out what went wrong can be a devilishly difficult task at that point.

A system is truly a set of pieces working together for the good of the learning goal. And this means that it is important that each step along the way is properly and precisely performed and that the

Figure 1.1 Well-fitting jigsaw puzzle    Figure 1.2 Ill-fitting jigsaw puzzle

outcomes of one step will properly feed the next step in the process. When we talk about systems in ID for classrooms, we are saying that the outcomes from each step *feed* the next steps, that they all fit together in a way that helps the entire endeavor to work properly in the classroom.

In order for classroom ID to work, it all has to fit together like a well-fitted jigsaw puzzle, not like a sloppily assembled jigsaw.

*Systemic Versus Systematic*

I would like to make a distinction here between systemic and systematic. This is a distinction I have made in the past (Carr, 1996) and one that I think is very useful here. Systematic is the easier to define, as it is a process that is usually linear, step by step and disciplined. Because of the nature of systematic processes, it may seem to be ill-matched to the fast-paced, dynamic, flexible nature of classroom life. A systemic approach is one that looks at the *whole* picture from a very high level to consider possible solutions. ID in the classroom needs to have a careful balance of both systematic and systemic approaches. The process needs to be clear and linear, particularly as you are first learning about the process. However, without the larger picture, the very narrow systematic approach will not be effective in the longer term. What this means for you is that you need to try to hold two things in your mind at the same time as you learn these steps. First, you need to understand the specifics of each step, how they work, how they fit together. It also means that you're going to learn these broader heuristics—or rules of thumb—that will help you to see the broad whole picture and you need to hold those bigger ideas in your mind at the same moment that you hold the more specific steps in your mind. Blending both *systemic* and *systematic* is a really wonderful way to get the best of both worlds for use in your own classroom.

*Obstacles*

While a well-fitted puzzle will make an excellent instructional moment in the classroom, there are definitely some hefty obstacles that may cause you to pause and wonder if ID in your classroom is the right way to go. The most common criticism of ID in the classroom among teachers is the amount of time that conducting the entire process may take. Where a brief lesson plan might take a few moments to complete, a complete instructional design blueprint or plan might take hours to complete for a single hour of instruction. There is no doubt that the way that ID fits into the classroom time-management schema for most teachers is the primary obstacle. We are interested in helping teachers overcome this criticism by offering heuristics which can be used in the moment. While a well-fitted puzzle might be needed for complex learning lessons, the notion that heuristics can be used in most cases on the fly in the classroom is one way to move beyond that criticism (see Figure 1.3).

In addition, there is a concern over the nature of the ID process as a *behavioral* one. And, in fact, it does work on the whole within a behavioral framework, meaning that the underlying notions of learning are those of information transmission rather than learner construction. I deal with this specifically by first showing you the basic behavioral model, and then sharing some ways that you can alter the model and work a constructivist[1] solution within the behavioral model. This is related to another broad category of concerns voiced by teachers who learn ID for the classroom. There is concern that ID just doesn't fit with the demands of today's classroom. Specifically, can ID work

**Figure 1.3** Variety of puzzles

with inquiry-based learning, student-centered learning, and, above all, standards-based curricula? Those, like me, who apply ID in classrooms believe it most definitely can be useful in these contexts and so I have provided separate chapters for each of these areas. Once you have the basic model and the heuristics well in hand, it's like a musician who can move from the theme to the variations on the theme. You will be able to take the basic model and adapt it for inquiry learning or constructivist learning environments.

In addition, there is a certain amount of fear that the ID for classrooms process will limit the "teachable moments" that you can take advantage of in the daily teaching experience. This is one of the most wonderful and fun parts of teaching, taking that moment when a child asks about the election as an opportunity to, in the moment, create a quick lesson on democracy based on their keen interest. This is a very important and exciting part of the teaching process, and it is certainly not the intent of ID for the classroom to take away that spontaneous and serendipitous moment. In fact, once you are able to master the process—and even more critically, the heuristics of the ID process—you will be able to create a much *better* spontaneous lesson because you'll quickly see the relationship of the goal with the test and the activities. We will revisit these obstacles in more depth near the end of the book after you have a bit more experience with the basic model and some of the variations on the theme as well.

*An Overview of the Model*

The ID for teachers (ID4T) model is a basic ID model, fashioned after the well-known models of ID from Dick, Carey & Carey (2009), Reiser & Dick (1996), Seels & Glasgow (1998), and many others who have come before me. These giants of the instructional design field all have many of the basic steps and ideas in the instructional design process in common. I've tried to boil these down into a sensible simplified process of creating learning for classrooms. Each of these steps will be considered in far more detail in Chapter 2.

The model can be nicely encapsulated in our model of a schoolroom (see Figure 1.4). The basic steps are as follows:

1. Write instructional goals.
2. Write learning objectives.
3. Write aligned assessment/test items.
4. Analyze learner characteristics/prerequisites.
5. Select materials/text.
6. Select and design activities.
7. Select (and develop if necessary) media/technology.
8. Implement the plan.
9. Evaluate and revise the instruction.

The first step, and the foundation upon which the entire experience is built, is *writing the instructional or learning goal.* This should be a concise statement of the point of the instruction. What is it that you want your learners to be able to know or do or feel at the end of the lesson?

The second step is to begin to break down the learning goal into *objectives.* Typically this overarching goal is made up of several smaller steps or pieces that the learning can be broken into. These should be carefully framed as learning objectives. What are the parts that make up the learning goal?

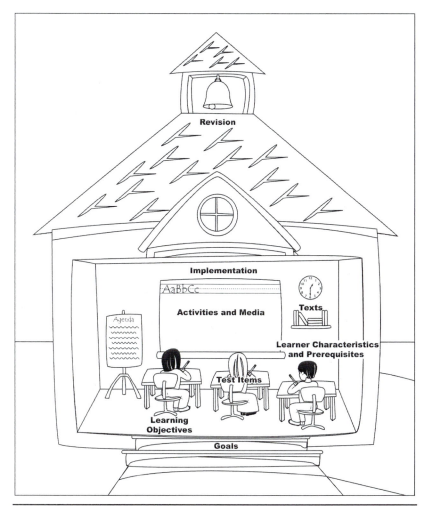

**Figure 1.4** The nine steps of the ID4T model

The third step is to *write test items* that match the learning objectives. Of course we should recognize the need to write good well-formed test items that really measure effectively—no more of the "gotcha" multiple choice questions. The point isn't to create a test that will sort learners, but a test that will measure whether or not your learners meet the learning goal and objectives. The most important part of this process is matching the test items to the learning goal and objectives.

The fourth step is to analyze the *learner characteristics/prerequisites*. This is made up of two basic notions: The first is who are your learners, what do they know, what do you know about them, and what learner styles do they respond well to? A deep understanding of the learner is essential for so many of the following steps. The second part of this step is matching those understandings with the objectives as you break them down into smaller and smaller sub-objectives until you reach a point where you're pretty sure that your learners are able to perform *that* objective. These are linked because you have to understand your learners and what they know and are already able to do in order to more fully understand the learner prerequisites.

The fifth step is to *select the materials* for the lesson. Which texts, posters, flashcards, or other *materials* (these are not media or technology which is dealt with later in the process) are well suited and useful for this learning goal and objectives?

The sixth step is to *select and design activities* that match the learning goal and objectives. To the extent possible, and appropriate, activities can and should mirror the actual expected behavior and possibly the assessment whenever the test is authentic and reflective of the test items. Thus, which activities will support your learners in mastering the learning goals and objectives?

The seventh step is *selecting and possibly developing media and technology*. This is a big step in that you first have to determine whether and what technology or media may be useful in supporting the activities you've selected in the prior step. Then, if that technology or those media don't exist in a useable way, you may have to edit a learning object to fit your needs, or develop something entirely new. Finally, once selected and/or designed, the media or technology needs to be effectively integrated into the lesson and larger classroom.

The eighth step is to *implement the plan*. This is the messy middle part that most ID models tend to avoid much discussion of. But paying attention to resources such as time, money, and people, as well as careful examination of the supports you'll need to effectively implement the instructional solution—be it administrative support, parent communications, additional funding, thematic units, or cooperation from teacher team members and colleagues—is essential to the final success of your plan.

The ninth and final step is to *evaluate and revise the instruction*. Note that this is different from student assessment, which would take place in the implementation step. However, the results of student assessments would definitely be an important part of the evaluation picture as well as several other measures of effectiveness. Identifying those areas that are not working well in the instruction, through systematic data collection, and then trying to fix them, can be promoted by careful one-on-one and small group trials of the instruction prior to complete implementation with a large group.[2]

## How to Use This Book

The easiest and most effective way to approach reading this book is for you to have in mind a *single hour* of instruction that you wish to design as you read and learn the planning strategies described in this book. Certainly you can simply read the book all the way through, or you can work through the book in a course or with a team of teachers in your school. If possible, try to work out the questions at the start of each chapter and write them down, and try out as many of the steps as you can along the way by using that one hour of instruction that you are interested in creating or improving. Take note of the "What you can do now" chapter summaries as a self-check to ensure that you feel confident that you've mastered the content in that chapter before moving on. This book does not assume that you already know a great deal about instructional design, and so will be useful even for a novice. But if you are already an expert or experienced designer, you may find that you can see the ways in which *this* model differs from others and you may theorize about why that makes sense in the context of classrooms.

You'll see boxes which will give rules of thumb for creating goal statements, learning objectives, media selection, and so forth. There are also boxes that illustrate common errors made when designing instruction with this model, and better possible solutions are given which will help you to follow these steps. Try to carefully study each step, and try not to tackle more than one step in a week's time. Take the time to learn about each step in detail and try it out with a couple of different lessons that perhaps you've been struggling to improve. Holding the heuristics and common errors in your mind at the same time is one of the best ways to understand ID for teachers more holistically.

You'll notice many examples and cases throughout the book to help make ID real for you. As you come to examples, try to see weaknesses or opportunities to improve the example before you read my feedback or suggestions to the student. As you read over the cases, try to apply the ideas to your own classroom, and think about how the experience might differ given your own content and context.

As Chapter 2 is such a long chapter, I would highly recommend you work through only one of the steps at a time. Give each step perhaps a week or so to sink in. Try the step out in your own classroom, with the instruction you're focused on right now. You'll find that the application of the model works very well when done in small chunks.

Once you have a pretty good grasp of the basics, focus on the heuristics and imagine yourself using that heuristic in two or three specific instances that happened to you this past week. This sort of personal projection can really help you to make the transition from the ideas and theories presented in the book into using them daily in the classroom.

### Learning Theories: a Primer

Understanding a little bit about learning theory is important here. I firmly believe that what *you* believe about how people learn (also known as your epistemology), and how they understand the world, impacts the decisions you make about instructional design. It will impact the choices of strategies, media, models, methods, and assessment that you're likely to select. Before explaining the ways in which learning theory might impact, let's *briefly* review the primary learning theories that exist. I have identified four very broad categories of ideas people have had about how learning happens. These have been written about by many well-known learning theorists (e.g., Schuman, 1996) and you can find out more about any of these should you wish to do so. I challenge you to learn more about one of the theories that may not align well with how you think learning happens, as investigating other theories can offer you a new perspective on learning and teaching.

The first theory is *behaviorism*. In essence, behaviorism is the idea that the mind is a black box and that knowledge is really best understood as observable behavior. We're not really that interested in understanding what happens in that black box, we just know that when we see the expected and desired behavior, learning has happened. Thus learning becomes about reinforcing the proper behaviors, extinguishing incorrect behaviors, shaping behaviors as they successively approximate the proper behaviors, and teaching becomes largely about the control of the environment. Skinner is the theorist most associated with behaviorism.

The second theory is *information processing or cognitive learning theories*. In these learning theories the mind is not a black box. Rather the mind is seen more as a computer or a file cabinet. Knowledge is seen as objects and the memory as a place that contains objects. The basics of this theory of learning are that it's all about an expert (teacher usually) figuring out how to map their knowledge onto the learner's existing knowledge. That "blank slate" or *tabula rasa* idea is central here, where you can imagine the learner as a vessel into which information is poured and learning happens when they are able to follow the rules and mirror the expert's performance. Thus they solve the addition problem correctly because they've seen the addition problem solved correctly, and they duplicate that.

The third theory is *constructivism*, particularly social constructivism.[3] Stemming from cognitivism, constructivist learning theories understand the mind as the inner representation of outer realities. Thus knowledge resides in the mind of the learner, and meaning then is internally constructed *by* the learner. This means, at its most radical, that all knowledge is created by the learner inside their head. Most constructivist learning theories understand reflection and abstractions as primary learning goals and the learning/teaching act is negotiated as meaning is constructed. The notion that the classroom is a social terrain where there is negotiation among all learners about what meaning is made is central to this learning theory. In addition, the primacy of active learning and problem-solving are both seen as good ways to engage learners in the construction of their own learning in this theory. In more recent times, the use of scaffolding[4] as a way to understand instruction within the constructivist learning environment has come into favor, as has the use of constructivism in certain learning situations regardless of personal epistemology or beliefs about learning. These less radical stances

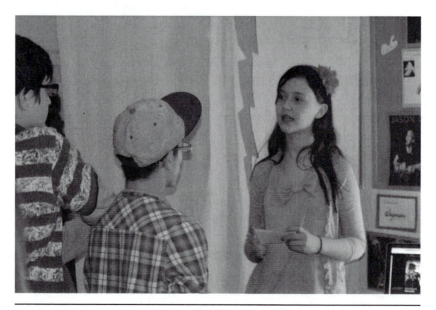

**Figure 1.5** Student-led learning. Photo by Jules Carr-Chellman.

on constructivist learning have led to a good deal more adoption of social constructivist notions in classrooms.

The final theory of learning is *postmodernism* in which the mind is seen as being in the world and thinking and living are both interpretation. Each individual is more a special case of a group rather than an. individual in him/herself. Social relationships often define individuals, considering that interactions among these individuals can define new knowledge and skills. Life is seen as a text and everyday life is the primary construct. This learning theory is rather on the leading edge of learning theories and is mostly embraced as part of a larger understanding of the existence of people in the postmodern world which emphasizes critiques of power and unquestioned constraints of modern life.

Knowing which of these or other learning theories most aligns with what you believe about learning and learners can help to guide you significantly into the future of your instructional design processes. You may feel that behaviorism works in some cases, like potty training, and constructivism in other cases, like higher-order learning. You may find that you believe absolutely that *all* learning happens in one way or another; after all, beliefs are rather personal and definitive things, in most cases. The purpose of sharing learning theories with you here isn't to ask you to concretize your beliefs about how learning happens, but rather to point out that these do lead naturally to certain types of goals, objectives, activities, and media choices. Thus starting here is not a bad plan.

Beyond understanding your position on learning theories, a clarity about the *type* of learning that you're approaching is essential. Without knowing the type of learning that you're aiming at, you're likely not to hit your target. In moving to a more concrete set of thoughts about learning, we can turn our attention from theories of learning to types of learning. Leshin, Pollock, & Reigeluth (1992) outline four types of learning: memorizing, understanding, applying, and higher-level thinking. Gagne (1965) has outlined five types of learning:

1. Intellectual skills include discriminations, concrete and defined concepts, rules and higher-order rules or problem-solving.
2. Verbal information is a lower-level set of skills including labels, facts, and organized knowledge.
3. Cognitive strategies include ways to better understand your learning such as rehearsal, elaboration, organizing, and comprehension monitoring.
4. Affective skills, commonly thought of as attitudes and appreciations.
5. Motor skills, which are the psychomotor or kinesthetic skills that are needed for various kinds of bodily performances.

## Conclusion

It is common to feel overwhelmed, challenged, excited, demoralized, angry, thrilled, and tired in one day in most classrooms in America today. As a teacher, your job is enormous. The trust that parents put into your hands when they put their little ones (and bigger ones) onto that bus each morning can be awe-inspiring. New programs, new initiatives, standards, new curricula, flagging budgets, inclusion of special needs children in your classroom, and parental demands can make the task of learning a new or slightly different way of planning seem mundane, unimportant, and distant. Please, spare a moment to take a deep breath and understand that learning ID will really be as much about allowing these ideas to "wash" over you as it will be in the detailed study of each individual step. Whenever you come to this book, I challenge you to take three deep breaths before reading anything, relax, and start to understand these ideas at a global level as well as within the details that they offer. As in one of those Magic Eye 3D pictures, you're likely to see all the details with diligent focus, but the larger systemic picture will be lost until you unfocus and allow yourself the freedom to really see what is here.

The rest of the book is structured in this way:

*The Basic Model (Chapter 2)*

This chapter is the "meat" of the text, focusing on the nine basic steps in the modified ID process for teachers. You may recall that analysis is all but eliminated, so the remainder of the process will include:

1. Setting learning goals.
2. Writing learning objectives.
3. Writing assessments/tests.
4. Analyzing student characteristics and entry level behaviors (prerequisites).
5. Selecting materials.
6. Developing instructional activities.
7. Selecting media.
8. Implementing the lesson.
9. Revising the instruction.

The systematic nature of these steps will be of great importance (that they all work together rather than as discrete steps) and the way that they build upon the outcomes of each step will be emphasized. This chapter introduces heuristics (rules of thumb) that can be easily recalled in the heat of classroom situations and applied, as well as common errors to help teach the basics of the ID4T model.

*How Does ID4T Really Work in*
*My Classroom? (Chapter 3)*

This chapter will address some of the current issues that are facing teachers in classrooms today, including No Child Left Behind and the ever-increasing calls for accountability. Other related school context factors will be addressed here. Pragmatic focus on the heuristics and common errors shared in Chapter 2 from the model itself will be re-emphasized in terms of how the model can easily be utilized in a daily fashion in the classroom, without taking 10 weeks to design a single unit of instruction from beginning to end. Two cases are offered to illustrate more concretely how the model is intended to work in the classroom in real ways.

*How Can We Integrate Constructivist*
*Notions into the ID4T Model? (Chapter 4)*

This model is based on, and similar to, several other fairly behavioral models, with a focus on clear goals and objectives for learning set out in advance. However, there are many classrooms that are now using, or trying to use, constructivist notions of learning in the classroom. Constructivism can seem, on the face of it, to be at odds with the traditional behavioral method of instructional design, and this is indeed the case. This chapter confronts the ways in which teachers can, in a daily way within their classrooms, create clear lessons that are of high-quality instruction while still using a constructivist foundation.

*How Can We Integrate User-Design*
*into the ID4T Model? (Chapter 5)*

User-design (UD) in the classroom implies empowering learners in significant ways. This is also seemingly at odds with the goal-setting by the teacher and the tendency toward expertism within traditional ID models. This chapter addresses ways in which UD can be a part of ID in the classroom by allowing the learners to select the goals and objectives where possible, and then creating effective high-quality instruction by thinking about these basic ID principles with the learners themselves.

*How Can We Integrate Inquiry Learning*
*into the ID4T Model? (Chapter 6)*

Inquiry learning, much like constructivism, is a model that has been very popular in recent years in classrooms, particularly in science learning. This chapter addresses ways in which inquiry learning can be integrated into the basic teacher ID model, with a particular emphasis on systemic alignment across the planned instruction to ensure that inquiry learning is the *appropriate* choice for the learning itself, and how to then go forward with high-quality instruction via ID4T.

*How Can I Use the ID4T Model with a*
*Standards-Based Curriculum? (Chapter 7)*

One of the most important accountability measures of the past decade, ushered in full force through the Bush administration's No Child Left Behind (NCLB) mandate, is a clear set of standards that each child must meet in order to be considered on grade level or successful. This chapter will address ways in which the model can be used in the face of standards and what sort of modifications must take place in order to effectively use the ID4T model in that setting.

*Using ID4T in the Online Classroom (Chapter 8)*

Online learning is an important and very popular form of learning that is entirely engaged within online settings. Content is distributed by computer typically via the Internet and this has significant implications for the ID4T model. This chapter will address ways in which the model can be used in the face of shifting needs of online learners. The chapter also addresses the potentials and challenges associated with online learning models.

*Using ID4T in the Flipped Classroom (Chapter 9)*

Flipped classrooms are an exciting new innovative happening in many schools across the country. The essence of a flipped classroom is one in which the instruction is happening at home or on the students' own time, and the "homework"— what we typically think of as homework—is happening in the classroom. This model makes the most of guided practice as an important cornerstone of learning. This chapter helps explain what a flipped classroom is, why they might be useful in some instances, and what methods within ID4T can be applied to flipped classrooms. In this chapter we differentiate flipped classrooms from traditional classrooms, particularly where media selection and text selection are concerned.

*Gaming and ID4T (Chapter 10)*

While most of us may imagine how fun games can be, using games in learning environments represents a new and important challenge. This chapter will help to guide you through the effective integration of games into your classroom. We explore how games can improve your classroom and what potential applications are available in gaming for learning. We look at what methods of the ID4T model are best applied to a gaming classroom, and what issues of media and text selection are important to consider when using games to learn.

*What Are the Primary Advantages and Drawbacks*
*of the ID4T Model for Teachers? (Chapter 11)*

Ensuring clarity and quality in instruction on a daily basis is a significant advantage of the use of ID for teachers, one that is very important, and yet obviously overlooked as so many teachers do not use ID in their own classrooms. Drawbacks of the model include the time investment required to ensure high-quality instruction and to truly engage the ID process; the loss of teachable moments; and the loss of natural integration across disciplinary areas. This chapter will expose these drawbacks and describe ways that teachers can mitigate these obstacles through the ID process rather than in spite of it. This chapter also shares a number of powerful motivators for using ID4T in the classroom, which helps to balance the obstacles and make it worthwhile to overcome them in order to unleash the power of ID4T.

*A note on charts* Chapter 2, where the model itself is presented, is illustrated with a large number of charts and documents. Some are from student projects (with their permission),[5] others are created from student materials but changed in format or context to help illustrate a variety of approaches at all levels of classroom practice. These charts are not the only way to array the information from these steps in the ID4T model. You should be creative in your own work and create charts and documents that work for you in your own ID process in your classroom. The charts are offered only as examples of one way that made sense to that particular teacher and shouldn't be seen as templates which should be copied. In some cases the charts illustrate common errors for you to learn from and may not always be the "best" or perfect example; instead they are a learning tool and should be thought of as such.

### What You Can Do Now (Chapter Summary)

At this point you will probably be able to:

- Define, in your own words, what instructional design is.
- Identify the basic steps in the process of instructional design.
- Describe the systemic and systematic nature of instructional design.
- Identify and discuss some of the obstacles to the use of instructional design in the classroom.
- Have a better sense of how the book is organized and how you can use it.

### Notes

1  If you are not familiar with the basic notions of behaviorism and constructivism, you'll find a more extensive discussion under "Learning theories: a primer" later in this chapter. Suffice it to say that behaviorists focus on the behavior that results from the learning and do not pay much attention to the process, whereas constructivists believe that learning is all created within the learners' minds and thus is constructed rather than transmitted.

2  *Instructor Note:* If you're familiar with these and other ID models, you'll see a few very distinct differences from what we think of as traditional ID models. The primary difference is that there is no real problem analysis. It is very common in corporate, higher education, and non-profit training contexts to pay careful attention to "what is the problem here?" This

question is one that is essential in these other contexts, because the problems might be related to job design, incentive systems, communication systems, and other non-instructional problems—what we call *performance technology*. However, in the classroom model, there is no real need for problem analysis. While it may be useful to consider the *relevance* of a given instructional unit, something that is particularly useful for student motivation, there is little need to consider something *beyond* or *outside of instruction*. In the classroom, formal instruction is almost assured as the solution to the learning goal. It is not really within the purview of most teachers to change salaries for their students, for example. Nor will job aids really work in a standardized testing situation, so many of the traditional performance technologies don't quite work in this environment. It may be constructivist, learner-centered, inquiry-based, problem-based or traditional, but it will almost certainly be a formal classroom solution. It is not really within the power of most teachers to change this reality, so there is no need to spend a great deal of time trying to understand the underlying performance problems and thinking about alternative solutions. Many instructional designers can find up to half of their efforts spent on problem analysis and needs assessment. So this part of the process is excluded from the ID for teachers model. For those readers who are really interested in learning more about ID as a broad discipline and one that can be applied to broader contexts than schools, or for those of you who really wish to tool up for the use of ID models in corporate, higher education, or non-profit settings, I encourage you to read Allison Rossett's (1987) *Training needs assessment*. Beyond this very large difference, you'll find that most of the differences between traditional ID models and this school-based ID model are really very small and are focused on making the model more useful for teachers on the front lines.

3  Note that the historical progression of these is not as simple as is presented here and can be traced in a variety of ways, but for our purposes it is presented in a more simplified fashion.

4  "Scaffolding" is a term overused and sometimes misused and so merits a brief definition here. Scaffolding in education refers to the use of specific supports such as graphics, modeling, motivation techniques, or activation of prior knowledge.

5  Thank you to Brendan Bagley, Jonathan Michael, Jennifer Landry, Bridget Fox, and Caitlin Conroy for agreeing to contribute portions of their final projects to this book project.

# 2

# What Is the Instructional Design for Teachers (ID4T) Model?

Chapter Questions

1. What are the basic steps in ID for teachers?
2. How are these steps different from other ID models?
3. What makes a good learning goal?
4. What are the important parts of a learning objective?
5. Why do you need to examine student characteristics before creating the instruction?
6. What are entry level behaviors? Why are they important?
7. What makes for a good test item?
8. What is test alignment?
9. What criteria should you use in selecting materials?
10. How should activities be selected?
11. How should media be selected?
12. What's the biggest danger in selecting media?
13. What new things should you consider when implementing a new lesson for the first time?
14. How should you go about revising the instruction?

Introduction

This chapter will present, in very simple, easy-to-understand language, the precise process that you should ideally go through each time you want to prepare a new lesson for some new content in your classroom. This is a *theoretical* model, which means that it is something that works pretty well in theory. However, understanding the real world of the classroom is a very different matter. The remainder of the book will deal with how the model works in a variety of situations in your real classroom, through standards, constructivist approaches, inquiry-learning models, and so on. But before we can understand the variations, we need to hear the theme of the music. How is the model *supposed* to work at its best? We'll talk about the good, bad, and ugly a bit later.

You will learn nine basic steps to good practice in instructional design. Even though you may feel that you could *never* do all of this for any unit of instruction in your classroom, or that it may change the teachable moments you enjoy in your current classroom, I encourage you to stay with it and learn the nine basic steps because these basic ideas will come back over and over again to you as you do the real work of preparing new lessons every day in your classroom. It may feel like it comes back in little ways, and I'm going to try to help you integrate these little ideas through heuristics throughout the chapter, sometimes with several for each step. These heuristics will help you use this model on the fly.

This may seem like a rather long chapter, but I feel that it's important to keep the whole model together because each step is related to the other steps, and builds upon the previous steps, so it is very important to keep all the pieces of this particular puzzle on the table at the same time. This connectedness is emphasized in this chapter as well.

One brief note here: This model is not at all unlike most other models that have been put forward for good instructional design procedures. There are lots of them out there, and they all sort of follow what is called the ADDIE process, which, again, stands for analysis, design, development, implementation, and evaluation. Basically, you first check out the situation, create a solution idea, make the actual solution real in some way, try it out, and see if it worked. It's not really any more complicated than that—it's common sense. However, understanding how these pieces can fit together and align is critical, and *integrating* these ideas into your everyday classroom practice is not so easy as the simple sentence written above may make it seem.

Of great importance is that you understand that for many who do nothing but instructional design, the analysis portion of these more traditional models is essential. In many cases, months, even years, are spent trying to figure out precisely what the problem is through intricate, expensive, extensive, and thorough analyses. In the case of classrooms, this is really an unrealistic step that has kept many teachers from breaking through and unleashing the power of instructional design in their own classrooms. This is because, for the most part, analysis has already been conducted in the case of classrooms in most schools today. Whether they are private or public, or charter, most school communities have, in one way or another, agreed on the prescribed outcomes for their learners. This has become the case even more with the No Child Left Behind legislation (2001) and increased standardization across the curriculum in the United States. As a result, I have dropped this analysis step from the standard model for ID for teachers, as Reiser & Dick (1996) have done before me. The main thing to understand is that if you move from a classroom setting into some other setting (a corporate, university, or not-for-profit context) they're likely to have a lot of thoughts about analysis and you might want to take a look at some of that, such as Allison Rossett's classic text, *Training needs assessment* (1987).

Other than the analysis section being left out entirely, the other thing that makes this model a bit different is that the approach is to help you learn to use the model in the classroom. By using heuristics (little rules of thumb), you can learn to apply these powerful ideas in your everyday experiences of teaching, instruction, lesson planning, and activity creation. Most models focus on a precise mastery of the steps in the model to the exclusion of how this will impact practice. This book gives you both, with a real focus on how to *use* the model effectively and quickly in your classroom every day. I sincerely believe in the power of instructional design to improve learning moments and so I want to make it as easy as possible for you to unleash that power in your own classroom. So, let's take a look at the powerful keys that unlock the potential of learning in your classroom—the basic ID for teachers model.

The nine steps are:

1. Set learning goals.
2. Write learning objectives.
3. Write matched test items.
4. Identify prerequisites and learner characteristics.
5. Select materials.
6. Create and specify learning activities.

7. Select media.

8. Implement and try out the instruction.

9. Evaluate and revise the instruction.

**STEP 1 Learning Goals**

A learning goal is a simple one-sentence statement that is a pesky little thing because it's simpler to imagine than to properly write. You probably already have a sense of what it is that you want the learner to learn. For example, you might want your students to be able to perform three-digit addition. Stop for a moment now, and imagine how you would write a single sentence to capture all that this learning goal encompasses.

---

 LEARNING GOALS COMMON ERROR
Overcomplicating the learning goal statement

---

You may have overcomplicated the learning goal. It's the most common reaction to writing learning goals. You may have said something like, "After having understood the process of adding two digits in columns along with carrying, the learner will add three digits to include carrying and lining up their numbers properly in columns." There's nothing really *wrong* with this, but it muddies the waters and tends to create more confusion for you and the learner. What is it that you *really* want them to do at the end of the lesson? Understand how to line up numbers? How to add them? How to carry? Is it two-digit or three-digit addition that you're focused on? If the learners don't have two digit, should you go back and spend the entire lesson reviewing two digit? It's in the learning goal after all.

*The best favor you can do for yourself when writing a learning goal and deciding on your focus is to make it clear and narrow.* Make sure that you know precisely what it is that you want your learners to know, believe, or be able to do when the lesson is done. *If you start with a muddy learning goal, you're likely to end up somewhere entirely different from where you'd intended.*

### The Beatitudes for Educators

Here is an interesting case of a pretty simple, powerful lesson by a well-known teacher—Jesus—which went a bit off track:

> Then Jesus took his disciples up on the mountain and gathered them around Him. And then He taught them, saying:
>
> "Blessed are the poor in spirit,
> Blessed are the meek,
> Blessed are the merciful,
> Blessed are you who thirst for justice,
> Blessed are you who are persecuted,
> Blessed are the peacemakers,
> Be glad and rejoice for your reward is great in heaven."
>
> And Simon Peter said, "Do we have to write this stuff down?"
> And Philip said, "Will this be on the test?"
> And Andrew said, "John the Baptist's disciples don't have to learn this stuff."
> And Matthew said, "When do we get out of here?"
> And James said "What if we don't know it?"
> And Bartholomew said, "Do we have to turn this in?"
> And Judas said, "When am I ever going to use this in real life?"
>
> Then one of the Pharisees, an expert in law, said, "I don't see any of this in the syllabus. Do you have a lesson plan? Is there an activity for each of the seven intelligences? Where is the study guide? Will there be any authentic assessment? Will remediation and extra credit be provided for those who did not meet class requirements so they can still pass?"
>
> And Thomas, who had missed the sermon, came to Jesus privately and said, "Did we do anything important today?"
>
> And Jesus wept.
>
> Adapted from (http://outofthejungle.blogspot.com/
> 2005/12/beatitudes-for-educators-warning.html)

This amusing little story is a useful one for our purposes. *It highlights how very important it is that instruction is guided by a deep understanding of the learner as well as the learning.* If you know your goal and your instruction well, you'll easily, if not patiently, be able to answer learner questions like those above. You'll know precisely what will be on the test; what is important enough to write down; why your learners need this even if someone else doesn't teach it; and how it is related to real-life applications. The goal of the instruction will help you to focus on the learning and the learner, and help to answer the needs that are expressed daily by the classroom experience. Of course, having clear goals won't stop all learners from ever asking if something is going to come up on a state test, but it will help to center you in a way that will help to keep you from weeping!

There are some helpful hints, maybe even rules (though not hard and fast), for writing good learning goals. The first is that you should avoid the use of "and" at all costs. "And" *almost* always means that you have *two* goals not just one. For example, "First grade students will recognize, repeat, and read the following four sight words in a book." OK, here you have *three* different things, "recognize, repeat, and read." Those are actually all pretty different things. You'd measure them in different ways (perhaps having them point, having them match, and having them vocalize). Thus "and" usually muddies up goal statements, so avoid it if at all possible.

Another good idea is to avoid the use of vague terms like "understand" or "know." These don't make good learning goals. If you start by saying, "The learners will understand the basics of electricity," where will you even begin? This is a very large goal, and it's not measurable. How will you know that they understand electricity? Your goal needs to be narrower, focused, and easily measured such as, "The students will hook up a basic single-circuit battery light."

On the other hand, another common error is to make too many specifications in your learning goal, such as the length of time or conditions under which the learning is to be performed. For example, "The students will hook up a basic single-circuit battery light correctly 80% of the time within 10 minutes of classroom exploration time." This is very clear, focused, and highly measurable; however, it tends to rope you in too much. *You need to have flexibility within the learning goal, and this level of specificity is really more called for within the learning objectives, which is the next step.* It's pretty common to start writing an objective instead of a learning goal, particularly if you're usually writing objectives in your classroom already. It's sometimes hard to try to back up to a higher level and still maintain clarity. So striking a good balance between focus and flexibility is what's called for here. You want to know with clarity and conviction what you're teaching in that moment and not become confused by either too little focus or too many details.

 LEARNING GOALS COMMON ERROR
Using an inappropriate verb

Another very common error is to use a verb rather carelessly. We've already talked about "understand" and "know" which are too vague, but you may use a more precise verb inappropriately. In thinking about what you want your learners to do, sometimes it's easy to just use a verb that first pops into your mind. For example, "Learners will identify the uses of space heaters." Now this sounds like a pretty good and clear learning goal; however, that is only true if you really want them to *identify*. If you actually want them to describe the uses, then "identify" will result in objectives that are at too low a level of learning (as in "recall") for the *real* learning you want them to accomplish. The point here isn't to always use a verb that is at a high level, for maximum flexibility, but rather it's to make sure that the verb you use in your learning goal is really the verb that you want. This is also a concern in objectives of course but, as we'll see, because this is a systematic process, with each part informing the next, errors early on become magnified until they are fixed. Often you'll find that you'll try one verb or one learning goal and discover that it doesn't really work and you have to go back and tinker with that goal before the objectives will really come together.

I recently read a book called *Sparks of genius* by the Root-Bernsteins (1999), that I thought did a really good job of giving us some more interesting and powerful creative thinking tools. Their 13 tools to spark imagination and creativity were observing, imaging, abstracting, recognizing patterns, forming patterns, analogizing, body thinking, empathizing, dimensional thinking, modeling, playing, transforming, and synthesizing. These are all really different sorts of verbs for thinking about learning goals, and while some of them can be categorized into the more traditional cognitive, affective, and bodily or kinesthetic goals, they shed new light in my opinion on how we might imagine the process of educational goal-setting. By and large these verbs wouldn't be all that useful for the objective writing process because they aren't quite specific enough and are really at a more global level. To learn more about these powerful learning goal terms, you should definitely read *Sparks of genius*. There also exist online many lists of verbs for learning goals and objectives. A simple web search will turn them up. Categorizing the verbs in learning outcomes is a good way to at least begin to target what you might like to use for your goal statement. For example:

- *Knowledge* goal verbs might include: label, define, list, describe, identify, name, match, select, recall, or state.
- *Comprehension* goal verbs might include: explain, discuss, convert, distinguish, extend, generalize, offer examples, infer, predict, or summarize.
- *Application* goal verbs might include: change, compute, demonstrate, discover, manipulate, modify, operate, predict, prepare, produce, relate, show, solve, or use.
- *Analysis* goal verbs might include: break down, diagram, differentiate, discriminate, distinguish, debate, illustrate, point out, relate, select, separate, or subdivide.
- *Synthesis* goal verbs might include: create, generate, categorize, combine, compile, compose, create, design, devise, rewrite, summarize, tell, or write.
- *Evaluation* goal verbs might include: determine, appraise, compare, conclude, criticize, justify, interpret, or relate.

One of my students did a really nice job of thinking about goal-setting a couple of years ago based on Nitko's (2004) text *Educational assessment of students*. Nitko encourages goal writers to make their goals student-centered, performance-centered, and content-centered, matching the learner's educational level, limited to the most important outcomes, and consistent with state standards. It's a little hard to imagine attending to *all* of these things at the same moment as we write our goals. However, it's good advice to consider holding as many of these issues in our minds as we can while we write our learning goal, the first step toward better learning.

*Sample* Table 2.1 shows a sample from a student project of a learning goal and my feedback.[1]

Table 2.1  Baseball learning goal with teacher feedback

| Goal | Student statement: Soft/baseball players will execute playing first base with proficiency | Teacher feedback: This goal came a long way from its first draft and a good deal of discussion was spent determining whether soft/baseball should be separated out and what proficiency might mean. Proficiency doesn't have to be specified until the objectives stage, but the author should have an idea of what this means to him. |
|------|------|------|

**STEP 2  Learning Objectives**

The second step in building good instruction is to clearly specify those things that make up the learning goal. You really can't specify the sub-steps in the goal until you have a clearly written goal statement. Thus this second step is dependent on the first one. Once you have the goal, then you can begin to figure out what the parts of that goal really are. In the earlier case of the battery circuit, for example, we might have several general sub-parts that we can turn into learning objectives. The learners may need to gather the supplies, construct a circuit in at least three different ways, and describe what happened that made their circuits work or not work. These may be the basic sub-steps in reaching the learning goal of hooking up a basic single-circuit battery light.

It's nice to think about the learning goal as the foundation and the objectives as the stones on that foundation but when we actually start to break things down, it looks a lot more like an organizational chart where the goal is at the top of the chart, as the leader or driver of the instruction, and then there are pieces of that goal which make it up that we need to list and then break them down further (see Figure 2.6). This sort of breaking down or learning analysis doesn't have to be complex, comprehensive, exhausting, or onerous. It's simply about making sure that you have a clear image of what makes up the learning goal.

Among the most common errors in writing good objectives is one we've already visited: Writing an imprecise objective because it uses an imprecise verb. Common examples are verbs such as "know" or "understand." It's nearly impossible to measure whether a learner knows or understands something, but we can see them demonstrate something, observe them apply a concept, or hear them discuss an issue. Thus selecting the proper verb is important both in goals *and* objectives.

 LEARNING OBJECTIVES COMMON ERROR
Using an inappropriate verb

Another of the things that I commonly see as errors in this part of the process is resisting breaking down procedures. For whatever reason, the easiest kind of learning to break down seems to create the most resistance to actually breaking it down. Procedures are usually things we do in a certain step-by-step manner to a final effect; for example, opening a bottle of wine. First you get a corkscrew—and selecting the proper tool can have several sub-steps—then you remove the foil wrapper at the top of the bottle, insert the corkscrew into the cork at the proper angle, twist the screw down into the cork until it is fully inserted, and then (depending on your corkscrew type) pull down on the "wings" of the corkscrew until the cork is just at the lip of the bottle. Finally, you tilt the bottle and remove the cork without allowing any cork pieces to fall into the wine. This particular example is one from a previous student of mine—and this student wanted to do everything *but* make that simple list. He talked at length about types of corkscrews, which is just one small part or step in the process. He ended up writing objectives on wine selection, discerning wine types, and so forth, rather than outlining the procedures of how to open a bottle of wine. Whenever this happens it usually means that the *goal* is not really capturing what the instructor *really* wants to have happen in the learning. Sometimes we have to then go back and re-examine the goal. This back and forth characteristic of the ID process is called *iterative*. It allows us the freedom (and at times, I'll admit, the aggravation) to go back and forth to the various steps to see if things are really working the way we want them to.

Objectives should have three parts: *condition, behavior,* and *criterion.* These three are very simple. However, they sound more simple than they really are. CBC is the easiest way to remember the three. My father, a physician, used to ask me whenever I had my blood drawn, "What was your CBC?" (In medical terms, a CBC is a complete blood count.) So I always think of the objectives as sort of the lifeblood of the instruction: beyond the foundation or skeleton of a clear learning goal, it's the objectives that really specify and make things go. I think as teachers we often believe that it's really the media or the lesson plans or activities that are the lifeblood of instruction, but for me it's really about the objectives. *In the objectives, we clearly specify the sort of behavior we expect of our learners at the end and this is what ultimately makes things work in instructional design.*

LEARNING OBJECTIVES HEURISTIC
Objectives are the lifeblood. CBC stands for condition, behavior, and criterion

Objectives may sound simple to construct, but like many of the early steps in the process, precision is essential. One common problem is trying to create objectives that really are two or three or more behaviors, what we call *compound objectives.* An example of this would be, "Given a button, thread, and shirt (*condition*) the learner will cut the thread, thread the needle, place the button, and sew the button on (*behaviors*) properly and securely within 10 minutes (*criteria*)." The primary problem with this objective is that it's really several objectives, some of which are probably sub-objectives (*objectives which are at a lower level or subsidiary to the main objective*).

LEARNING OBJECTIVES COMMON ERROR
Using compound objectives (more than one behavior)

These compound objectives can be rather tricky, such as, "Given a photo book layout (*condition*) the learner will download photos in order to create a completed photo book (*behaviors*) with an attractive layout as judged by the creative director (*criterion*)." Often we see "in order to" or "so that" as flags which will indicate a second behavior. The "and" is an easy flag to see within a behavioral statement which almost always indicates two behaviors. The problem with having more than one behavior is simply that it tends to confuse and cause us to lose proper focus. We may be including sub-objectives; we may be including the learning goal, or a higher level objective; or we may be including an objective that is really a prerequisite to learning the final objective. Regardless, it will tend to cause confusion and lack of focus, so *it is imperative that you generate objectives that are focused on a single behavior. And it is perfectly OK to generate many objectives.* While it is important to figure out at what level the objectives are (which are subsumed under which other objectives), or what their relationship to one another is, it's also vital that properly formed objectives are fleshed out, each one individually.

*Parts of the Objective: CBC explained*

The *condition* is quite simply the way that the *behavior* is done. Under what conditions? We typically think of this as a list of "givens." Thus, "Given the proper wine opener and a bottle of corked wine, . . ."

 **BEHAVIORAL OBJECTIVES COMMON ERROR**
Teaching through your objectives

One of the most common things we see when writing conditions is using the conditions to begin imagining what the classroom will be like and therefore teaching *through* your objectives. For example, a condition such as "Given a roleplay and lecture, . . ." or "Given an understanding of basic physics, . . ." or "Given students' own research and background, . . ." are all common misuses of conditions in behavioral objectives. In the first case the condition is really talking about what the instructor intends to *do* with the class time—it's specifying an activity or learning strategy. There are two problems with this. First, the condition is supposed to help us think about how the final *performance* or behavior will look. So when creating a commercial, for example, what does a graphic artist need? A computer? A pitch from a client? Past ad campaigns? *What are the inputs?* Thus, the first common problem is that a condition might not accomplish its purpose to help us imagine the performance. The second common problem is that it assumes all sorts of things about the instruction which haven't yet been decided. This is one of the first times that you will face a recurring problem, a tendency that we all have to jump to imagining what will happen in the instruction rather than focusing on the single step we're in for that moment. It is a bit of Zen here to just sit and do one thing to its natural end and not to jump ahead of ourselves. In this age of multi-tasking it's very difficult *not* to get ahead of ourselves and think in multiple layers all at once, but I would suggest it is much more useful to learn the process of disciplined instructional design by taking one small piece at a time and weaving each one together one by one. So avoid this early error of teaching through your objectives, particularly in your condition statements.

The second and third errors are less common but are equally as problematic. The second problem is actually putting your prerequisite skills, or those things that your learners must know *before* they get into your lesson, into your conditions. So suggesting that the learners should just understand some critical prerequisite will mask the importance of careful analysis of the learning into its component parts and creation of pre-tests or linkage to prior learning. The third error is some combination of the prior two, both a reliance on the student's own prior knowledge or work as well as a direction for basic homework. These are not performance conditions. They are all errors in writing objectives and they tend to lead to teaching *through* your objectives instead of a careful analysis of the learning. At this point in the process, you should avoid jumping to the instructional moment and try hard to keep that image out of your head.

BEHAVIORAL OBJECTIVES COMMON ERROR
Forgetting or simplifying your criteria

Another very common error in writing good objectives is to completely forget to include a criterion which will tell you and your learners what will qualify as adequate performance or mastery of the objective. Likewise, if you oversimplify your criteria to just say that the learner will do something "correctly," "properly," or another general adverb, you are not really looking carefully at how well you want someone to perform the objective. When I was working at McDonnell Douglas creating training for jet fighter pilots, we had the luxury of time and money to spend on creating excellent training. However, at one point the management did not want to spend the necessary money for the instructional designers and subject matter experts to sit together and figure out to what level of performance each objective needed to be performed. So we had to figure out a shortcut. The quality assurance folks wanted us to put in some adverbs, basically at random, and one of our programmers created a "random adverb generator" to include three random adverbs into each objective written for an enormous helicopter training program. Obviously this was not a good solution because it did not match the objective with the criteria for judging its performance. Criteria need to be closely matched, so we think of criteria as "within 5 minutes" or "correctly solving 12 of the 15 problems." Less desirable is a general 80% proficiency.

One thing people sometimes become confused about here is the need for 80% versus 100% proficiency in most objectives. While we want to hold all our learners at a very high standard, 100% is not very realistic and does not really indicate mastery, but some level of automaton reaction. We want learners who can distinguish and properly perform the objective with thoughtful performance. That means that sometimes they'll make mistakes, so in general we accept 80% as mastery. However, in high-risk training such as medical training, firefighter training, emergency medical services (EMS) or other emergency training, flight training, and so forth, you'll want a 100% performance rate because it is so critical. Most things in schools do not require higher than 80% mastery and this does not mean that you have low expectations for your students, but that you're setting a reasonable rate to judge their performance as acceptable and the skill as mastered.

One other note here on the use of objectives with learners. We'll discuss this later in the text as well, but it's important to understand that the CBC format is for your use as a teacher, not for your use with students. Students will react far better when seeing clearly worded objectives that tell them what is needed but not in technical jargon-filled language. Thus you'll want to consider carefully rewording your objectives when using them with learners.

So what are the keys to an outstanding objective? They are a clear single behavior sandwiched between a condition for performing that behavior and a criterion for measuring that behavior—CBC.

*Sample* From the baseball example in Table 2.1, we see the development of the goal into the objectives alongside my critique of each objective (Table 2.2).

**Table 2.2** Baseball objectives with teacher feedback

| | STUDENT OBJECTIVE | TEACHER FEEDBACK |
|---|---|---|
| Objective | Given a standard base (1st base on a standard soft/baseball field) and a fielder's glove, the 1st baseman will demonstrate that the ball is hit to them or not by saying aloud "yes" or "no," and do it correctly 4 out of 5 times. | We never want to see "and" in the objective. Commas could be used to avoid this problem, but it is not crucial in the condition here. The behavior is quite clear, "demonstrate," and the means, "saying aloud," is also clear. The criterion of 4 out of 5 is appropriate as 100% is not needed for anything other than high-risk training. |
| Objective | Given a standard base (1st base on a standard soft/baseball field) and a fielder's glove, the 1st baseman will start in a position 2 feet from the base and facing home plate and will then after being signaled, immediately properly position him/herself to receive a thrown ball 4 out of 5 times. | The first objective is to identify if the ball is coming your way. The second objective is proper positioning. It may be that in terms of order, these two should/could be reversed, but it's not essential, it just seems to flow better. Clearly this objective can be nicely broken down into sub-objectives about proper positioning. |
| Objective | Given a standard base (1st base on a standard soft/baseball field) and a fielder's glove, and a player/coach hitting a ball to players other than the first baseman, the 1st baseman will position her/himself in their defensive position and then move to the correct receiving position by the time the ball is thrown to them 4 out of 5 times. | Now we have hitters in the picture. You'll note the inconsistency across the use of first baseman or 1st baseman. Consistency is better, but this is a minor problem. The larger problem here is that it's really two objectives "position" and "move to the correct receiving position." These should probably be two objectives. |

*(continued)*

**Table 2.2** Continued

| | STUDENT OBJECTIVE | TEACHER FEEDBACK |
|---|---|---|
| Objective | Given a standard base (1st base on a standard soft/baseball field) and a fielder's glove, and a player/coach hitting a ball to players other than the first baseman, the 1st baseman will make contact with the base with the correct foot while in the process of receiving the throw 4 out of 5 times. | Here's a really hard skill, and it's another compound objective involving both making contact and receiving the throw. Using "while in the process of" is true to the experience, but they are still two objectives. It could pass, but at minimum it would need to be clearly cut into two sub-objectives. |
| Objective | Given a standard base (1st base on a standard soft/baseball field) and a fielder's glove, and a player/coach hitting a ball to players other than the 1st baseman, the 1st baseman while in the contact with the base, and after the ball is thrown, will predict the direction of the throw by saying aloud, "straight," "left," or "right" correctly 4 out of 5 times. | Again this may be a compound objective. More discussion with the author may clear this up as it is possible that it really is just one action, but it seems to be involving two things. It is clear, however, in terms of the expectations, conditions, and criteria. |
| Objective | Given a standard base (1st base on a standard soft/baseball field) and a fielder's glove, and a player/coach hitting a ball to players other than the first baseman, the 1st baseman will disengage their foot from the base within 2 seconds after receiving the ball 4 out of 5 times. | This one is great! It is clear and other than having "and" as well as the inconsistent use of 1st baseman, this is really well done. |
| Objective | Given a standard base (1st base on a standard soft/baseball field) and a fielder's glove, and a player/coach hitting a ball to players other than the 1st baseman, the 1st baseman will distinguish, after the ball is thrown, if he/she needs to stay on the base or not (in the case of a poor throw) by saying aloud, "on" or "off" correctly 4 out of 5 times. | Again this one is clear, and while it's long, it is not a compound objective. |
| Objective | Given a standard base (1st base on a standard soft/baseball field) and a fielder's glove, and a player/coach hitting a ball to players other than the first baseman, the 1st baseman will catch/receive the ball that is thrown to them in the air within 3 feet to their left or right, 4 out of 5 times. | This is also really good and the author has wisely dropped the "correctly" from the criteria because this is an either/or, you catch or you don't, you receive or you don't. If more subtle correctness were to be added, it might be hard to judge properly. |
| Objective | Given a standard base (1st base on a standard soft/baseball field) and a fielder's glove, and a player/coach hitting a ball to players other than the 1st baseman, the 1st baseman will prevent the poorly thrown ball, within 3 feet of them, from going past them, 4 out of 5 times. | Again this one is very well written and clear. |

## STEP 3 Testing

> A key aspect of task analysis is aligning goals for learning with what is taught, how it is taught, and how it is assessed (both formatively and summatively). Without this alignment, it is difficult to know what is being learned.
>
> Committee on Developments in the Science of Learning,
> 2000, p. 151

Writing good tests is often a very charged experience. All of us can recall the awful feeling—that pit in our stomachs—when the teacher would announce, "Please take out a clean sheet of paper, there'll be a short quiz." Few of us really liked to take tests, though preparing for tests and taking tests is an essential part of any good instructional program and ultimately critical for learning. We have to overcome this initial block and avoid using test banks that may have been handed to us along with the curriculum for the year. It is surprising how out of alignment the tests and objectives can be in most vendor-provided curricular materials. *Testing is essential, but what is critical in the creation of good tests is a clear and complete alignment between test items and objectives.* This means that the test should present the exact condition named in the objective, and it should elicit the exact performance, and hold the same criteria as iterated in the objective. This sounds simple enough, but is remarkably difficult. It is not as difficult, I've found over the years, as creating well-written, comprehensive, appropriate learning goals and objectives; however, it can be trickier than you might think.

TEST ITEMS HEURISTIC
All test items must align in condition, behavior, and criterion with the objectives

There are many issues associated with testing: What is the role of intelligence quotients (IQ) and other standardized tests? Should I use multiple choice or fill-in-the-blank, or essay tests? How do I know if the test is working? Can the test tell me something about how to improve my instruction or is it more a reflection of the learners' ability to attend, or perhaps the breakfast they ate that morning?

There are few simple answers to these questions, but there are some rough heuristics or guidelines that we can begin to follow.

First, the test question type (multiple choice, essay, etc.) should be made based on the behavior that you are asking for in the objective. So if you're asking the learner to list, then you shouldn't use a multiple-choice question because you're giving them the list in the question choices. You're asking them, then, to select instead of list. If you want them to distinguish between several options, then a multiple choice may make sense. A compare-and-contrast task should probably be carried out through a written essay as that's almost impossible to assess with a fill-in-the-blank test item. If you ask the learner to discuss, then you'd better be prepared for an oral exam, and in that case it is best to prepare a rubric[2] for yourself as you go through the oral exam or the discussion (if you plan to assess as a group[3]). But be careful that you are not planning to teach through your test. Just as with your objectives, if you anticipate doing a class discussion and you plan to assess the learners as they are discussing, you have to be careful that you aren't jumping ahead of yourself and actually assessing the *instruction* instead of the learning. In such a case a rubric that could guide you through the discussion would probably be a useful artifact, but it would be difficult to assess the learner's final performance, and so it may be best to orally examine the learners individually.

Second, IQ and other standardized tests can be useful, but only as a snapshot glimpse into the students' abilities and they shouldn't be over-emphasized. For most of us, we can have access to some pretty powerful tests such as IQ, running records from prior years, and other standardized scores. We should be cautious about using those scores as definitive predictors of success or indicators of ability. While these tests are indeed rigorously vetted for reliability and validity, there are many learners who do not do well on the tests, but do very well in other kinds of learning environments. This discussion inevitably leads to a conversation about tracking and the extent to which tracking is a fruitful educational practice.

In general, I do not think that tracking or ability grouping is ultimately as productive or efficient as most of us might think. The primary purpose of tracking is to allow us to put children of like abilities into a group together. Most agree that 60% of elementary students and two-thirds of high school students are tracked or ability grouped (Hopkins, 2004). The basic idea here is that by putting like learners together, we will be able to teach the content that is at the proper learning or instructional level more efficiently. Csíkszentmihályi (1996) and Vygotsky (1978) do an excellent job of explaining to us how important it is to hit that sweet spot in learning, a place where the material is sufficiently challenging to be able to really motivate and engage learners. If the learning is too hard, the learner will give up out of frustration; if it is too easy, the learner will lose interest quickly. In seeking that perfect learning moment, we see that it makes sense for learners who are likely to hit that spot together to work in small teams. The most classic case of this is the leveled reading groups, which currently often begin in kindergarten. So given this, then, tracking makes sense, right?

Figure 2.1  Student use of technology for project-based learning. Photo by Jules Carr-Chellman.

Well, this sort of ability grouping or tracking can be extremely anti-productive because of the social pressure felt by the "redbirds" who know, quite clearly, that the "bluebirds" are smarter than they are, and that the "eagles" are the smartest in the class. Recognizing this, learners learn exactly what we're teaching them, that we don't think that they are as bright as others even when they are at such an early developmental level that they really cannot be classified in this strict tracking system with any real reliability or validity. They quickly learn to hate school, resist learning, and are quickly lost to the joys of new intellectual challenges. In addition to this primary drawback, it is well recognized that ability groupings are usually determined from subjective judgments, which are unreliable and, at young ages, highly elastic (Wheelock, 1992). Naturally, ability groups can create self-fulfilling prophecies for teachers and learners as well as place children based on the *pace* of their learning, rather than their actual abilities, or place them based on their levels of *compliance* abilities rather than their cognition. Finally, while we know that learners' abilities are highly variable and developmentally flexible, the stability of early tracking is remarkably static. Early tracking represents a stable artifact of early school judgments, which are not likely to be representative of children's actual abilities or learning zones of proximal development. Thus, while tracking may appeal in the short term, in the longer term it can be harmful (Wheelock, 1992).

Perhaps the most illustrative of the issues associated with too much or the wrong kind of testing, too many standards, and too much tracking, is the purple-fruit picking parable:

*The purple-fruit picking parable*

Statureland is an island nation with one major industry: purple fruit. Since purple-fruit picking is essential to the welfare of the whole society, the Statureland schools' basic curriculum is intended to train effective purple-fruit pickers.

Because purple fruit grows only at the top of eight-foot trees, the most important and critical course within the curriculum has been Growing. All children are required to take Growing, and they are expected to complete six feet of growth—the minimum criterion for graduation as purple-fruit pickers and the average height of Staturelandians, based upon standardized growing tests.

The course content of Growing includes stretching, reaching, jumping, tiptoeing, and thinking tall.

Each year, each child's skill and abilities in growing are assessed, and each child assigned a grade. Those children who achieve average scores on the standardized growing test are assigned B and C grades. Students who, through their commitment to growing, exceed expected levels, receive As.

Slow-growing students receive Fs and are regularly and publicly admonished for their lack of effort and inattention to the primary task. These latter children often develop poor self-images and antisocial behaviour that disrupts the school program and interferes with children who really want to grow.

"This will never do!" said the people. "We must call a wise man to consider our problem and tell us how to help the children grow better and faster and become happy purple-fruit pickers."

So a wise man was sent for and he studied the problem. At last, he suggested two solutions:

1. Plant pink-fruit trees that grow only five feet tall, so that even four-foot students may be successful pickers.

2. Provide ladders so that all students who wish to pick purple fruit can reach the tops of the trees.

"No, no, no!" said the people. "This will never work. How can we then give grades if eight-foot trees are goals for some students and five-foot trees are goals for other students? How can it be fair to the naturally tall students if children on ladders can also stand six feet tall and reach the purple fruit! However shall we give grades?"

"Ah," said the wise man, "you can't. You must decide whether you want to grade children or have fruit picked."

Reprinted from *CCPA Education Monitor*, Fall 1998

The point of this parable and my concerns regarding tracking are really about *what we do with the results of* assessments. While tests present many challenges to us in terms of issues associated with schooling today from standards to tracking, *the primary lesson of this model is that test items must align clearly with the objectives.* One of the most common errors made when creating tests is to find a random fact or discussion that happened in class and test on that. It is very common for us as teachers to go back in time in our minds and think, "Hmm, what could I write quiz items for from the Ancient Turkey unit?" What proceeds from this re-thinking of previous class time tends to be a mismatch between what the teacher may recall as important and what the learners may recall as important. Because you have created objectives, you have a target to shoot for and you need to focus on that target and hit it with the test items. If your learners feel that the questions are random, you can point to the objectives and show the alignment between them and your goals and objectives, and it will be clear that the test items are closely aligned. If you are trying, however, to figure out a good way to sort the kids into groups roughly based on the test's assessment of their abilities, rather than their mastery over the specific content, then you're likely to be frustrated by this sort of testing.

 TEST ITEMS COMMON ERROR
Choosing random test items rather than well-aligned test items

*Samples* There is a wide variety of ways that tests can be constructed, from check sheets to multiple-choice tests. The key here, of course, is to carefully align the test items and their format to the actual objectives and to what you really want the learner to be able to do at the end of the instruction. One of the reasons why this occurs so early in the process is to help form the remaining portions of the instructional design along the lines of the objectives and test items.

We'll start by looking back at the baseball example. I am not including all the ways that tests can be constructed in Table 2.3, just a couple to give you a sense of what the test "check sheet" contained. Once again, this part of the design document remains overly complicated, though well aligned. There is a good bit of redundancy with the prerequisite plans as well as unnecessary detail. You really want to have only the needed check sheet item, as shown in Table 2.4.

Table 2.3 Baseball test check sheet

| OBJECTIVE, TYPE, TEST ITEM, CHECK SHEET ITEM | YES | NO |
|---|---|---|
| 1. Given a standard base (1st base on a standard soft/baseball field) and a fielder's glove, the 1st baseman will demonstrate that the ball is hit to them or not by saying aloud "yes" or "no" and do it correctly 4 out of 5 times. | | |
| Objective 1: Intellectual skills—statement | | |
| Test item: The player will identify if the ball is coming toward them by saying "yes" or "no" aloud. | | |
| Check item: Did the player properly identify if the ball was coming toward them by saying aloud "yes" or "no" 4 out of 5 times? | | |
| 2. Given a standard base (1st base on a standard soft/baseball field) and a fielder's glove, the 1st baseman will start in a position 2 feet from the base and facing home plate and will then, after being signaled, immediately properly position him/herself to receive a thrown ball 4 out of 5 times. | | |
| Objective 2: Motor skills—checklist | | |
| Test item: Move to the starting position and then move into the proper receiving position. | | |
| Check item 1: Did the player begin by facing home plate? | | |
| Check item 2: Did the player see/hear the signal to move toward first base? | | |
| Check item 3: Did the player move to the proper position to receive the ball 4 out of 5 times? | | |

Table 2.4 Improved baseball test check sheet

| PERFORMANCE | YES | NO |
|---|---|---|
| Did the player properly identify if the ball was coming toward them by saying aloud "yes" or "no" (tally 4 out of 5 times)? | | |
| Did the player begin by facing home plate? | | |
| Did the player see/hear the signal to move toward first base? | | |
| Did the player move to the proper position to receive the ball (tally 4 out of 5 times)? | | |

Again, this is a much cleaner way for the teacher to be able to quickly see and mark performances. You'll also note that the test items are going beyond the objectives slightly, thus proper position is now being specified in the test items. This means that sub-objectives should be fleshed out in order to support those test items. Otherwise, it is possible that the learner will not know what it is that he/she is to be checked on since it is not explicitly stated in the objectives for the lesson.[4]

Figure 2.2 shows another example from a student project in which the goal was to build a computer. The instructional designer decided on a motor skills checklist (see Figure 2.3) as with the baseball example. I'd like to see this in a slightly more graphic representation such as is shown in Figure 2.4. Simplifying the language doesn't lose anything for the instructor and will be easier to check off when in the heat of the moment of evaluation/assessment.

A more traditional example of what test items might look like is shown in Figure 2.5. Note that the objective calls for the learner to "write" the expression, and the test items ask for the same thing. We would be likely to see multiple-choice items when the objectives ask

Given external power cables and power, students will test their computer by turning it on. The computer should turn on 80% of the time after repeated trials.

**Figure 2.2**  Computer build objective

1. Were there two power cables connected to the monitor and desktop?
2. When students turn on the computer, does the computer boot to the operating system?

**Figure 2.3**  Computer build test checklist

✓ Two power cables connected to the monitor and desktop?
✓ Computer boots to the operating system?

**Figure 2.4**  Improved computer build test checklist

**OBJECTIVE 1.  Given a balanced chemical equation, students will write an equilibrium constant expression correctly 80% of the time.**
1. Write the equilibrium constant expression for the following reaction:
   $N2(g) + {}^3H2(g) \longleftrightarrow {}^2NH3(g)$
2. Use the following chemical equation to write the equilibrium constant expression for the reaction:
   $HNO2(aq) + NaOH(aq) \longleftrightarrow Na^+(aq) + NO^{-2}{}_{(aq)} + H2O(l)$
3. A general equation of the form $aA + bB \longleftrightarrow cC + dD$ can be written for any chemical reaction. Write the equilibrium constant expression for this general chemical equation.

**Figure 2.5**  Chemical equilibrium test items

for memory recall, and matching items when the objective asks the learner to match or distinguish items.

**STEP 4  Learner Characteristics and Prerequisites**

Now that we have a fairly clear idea of what it is that we want our learners to do at the end (the goals and objectives), it's time to make sure we know our learners well and what will help them to reach those goals and objectives.

*The first step in understanding what our students are capable of is finding out what they already know, how they learn, and who they are.* Knowing your audience, or your learners in this case, is critical to overall success in creating effective instruction. For this purpose, we'll consider several important steps:

1. Break down the knowledge into its component parts.
2. Continue to break down the knowledge into its parts until you reach a point where you're sure the learners will already know that piece of it (ability to read, add simple sums, measure with ruler, for example).
3. Analyze your learners to find out what motivates them, how they learn best, what past experiences they bring to the learning, what cultural or individual factors may impact their learning.

In order to accomplish this first step, you need to take the first learning objective and start thinking about what it is that makes up the behavior. If, for example, you are explaining how to create a dovetail joint in wood shop, your first objective may be to distinguish dovetail joints from all other non-dovetail joints 80% of the time when looking at photos of various kinds of wood joints. In order to recognize joints, students will need to differentiate between joints. So what is that differentiation behavior made up of? Well, they have to be able to see the photos first (we can assume that's probably a prerequisite), meaning it's something that falls into step 2 and it's simple enough that we expect most learners in our population to be able to do it. Now if this was for special needs learners, we might have a different situation, but assuming a standard high school wood shop population, we would anticipate all of them would be able to see photos on a paper and visually be able to decipher them. Thus we break down the learning within the objectives into component parts as shown in Figure 2.6.

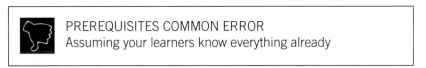

**Figure 2.6** Objectives hierarchy

> **PREREQUISITES COMMON ERROR**
> Assuming your learners know everything already

In addition to seeing the joints, the students have to attend specifically to the joints as opposed to other parts of the photo. So we should make sure that they then know what a joint looks like. They don't need to know how to define a wood joint, but they should be able to label it on a drawing or similar photo. This then becomes a sub-objective, "Given a photo of a wooden drawer with the joint showing, the learner can label the joint with 80% accuracy." There are likely to be many more similar sub-objectives; they are the meat of what makes up the performance of the objective. You have to keep breaking these sub-objectives down until you reach the point that you're pretty sure your learners will already know that particular nugget of content. In this case, it could be that they'll know how to label a joint, but they may not. If you cannot be certain that they know it, how will you find out?

Typically a pre-test will help to show what your learners already know; a brief check will tell you whether or not you may need significant remediation prior to instruction. Such a probe can be administered a session or two before the planned instruction. But where does that test come from? Be careful here, it's important that we do not assume we can just go out and create a survey or a pre-test off the top of our heads and it will work. No, it needs to be a careful explication of the content and behaviors into the sub-and sub-sub-objectives until you reach a point where you want to test to make sure that the students have the various prerequisite skills. Some of them may require a review at the start of the lesson, but for the most part, you should be able to have a clear picture of your learners' abilities in relation to the objectives and ultimate learning goal once you have given the pre-test.

PREREQUISITES COMMON ERROR
Creating a pre-learning survey without first doing a complete learning analysis of the objectives

At the same time, there may be some things that you know about the learners, such as what motivates them; what makes learning about wood joints relevant to their lives; do they learn better with pictures or spoken words; what are their favorite pastimes; why are they in your class; and so forth. You have to decide for yourself what are the relevant factors in your own instruction. You don't really need, or for that matter want, to know everything about their lives. But knowing about the kind of learning styles that are sitting in those seats in your classroom may be critical to successful instruction. You may find that a few additional items on a prerequisite skills test will shed a great deal of useful light on your planning as you learn about your learners.

At the end of this step you'll have a clear picture of your learning and your learners, you'll know in detail the specific skills, sub-skills, and prerequisite skills that are needed to achieve your learning objectives and ultimately your goal. You'll know a great deal about the learners as well and it will help you to create appropriate activities, and select the right media.

*Samples* Identification of prerequisites is typically not done in a chart format or with graphic representations. Figure 2.7 shows an example of a butterfly lesson at the elementary level.

Some designers find that a survey can give a great deal of information about the learners, and this data can sometimes be contrary to

**LESSON PREREQUISITES**

1. Read butterfly vocabulary from word bank

*Pre-assess reading:* Fountas & Pinnell running records to assign instructional level; IEP[5]/Title I findings
Reinforcing vocabulary before lesson: a teacher-created word wall helps connect new concepts with prior knowledge. Using previous vocabulary words helped form a foundation for the new lesson. The class reviewed the definitions and discussed the importance of these words in the new lesson. New vocabulary was added to the color-coded word wall after students used their own words and drawings to record meanings in their journals.

2. Understands how to arrange events in sequential order; knows what sequence means

*Pre-assessment:* formal assessment: sequencing worksheet (i.e. put these pictures in order; first, next, finally)—mastery with this worksheet determined their readiness to complete the sequence lesson objective; informal assessment: questioning, large/small group response to sequence activity

3. Motor skills: ability to hold a pencil and manipulate images to sequence

*Pre-assess:* teacher observation from previous lessons and completion of similar objectives on previous lessons was means of assessing. None of these students have an IEP or 504 plan that includes physical therapy for motor skills. Each of these students is able to draw, cut, color, etc., at an ability level matching my objectives.

4. Assumes students have some prior knowledge of butterflies and are not afraid of photographs of them

*Pre-assess prior knowledge:* Asked students to complete a K-W-L chart; as a group we compiled a class T-chart of "What the students know" and "What the students want to learn" about butterflies.

*Pre-supposed attitude:* I assume all students in this classroom are familiar with butterflies and are not afraid of them. Pre-assessment included integrating leveled readers into RELA small groups to determine if the accompanying close-up photographs/illustrations made anyone uncomfortable. Informal assessment during KWL and book activities to check for squeamish.

*Pre-supposed learning style:* Instruction and assessment are primarily visual (interactive whiteboard) and a drawing objective. In addition to directed questioning of students who had previously been found to be kinesthetic or auditory learners, I also include sound and video in my files to engage and redirect those learners. I would administer an interest inventory, a learning styles pre-test, and data from informal observations to help decipher my students' learning styles.

*Pre-supposed physiological characteristics:* Will the time of day (energy levels/ food and drink/mobility) affect how students learn? Science is right after morning recess and one student has a difficult time winding back down to get into the zone of learning. I observed the students to assess if they were ready to begin or if they brought a playground matter back into the classroom. By starting the lesson with a good anticipatory set (a huge pupa), and beginning the lesson with a short story about butterflies, I helped this student (and any others in the class) refocus themselves. This student was formally evaluated by me and another classroom teacher, as well as the guidance counselor and his parents, using the Connors questionnaire. At that time he was found to have attention deficit concerns.

*Pre-supposed environment characteristics:* Are any students affected by sound, light, temperature, and furniture/setting design? Previous teacher observation of student behavior determined if students had special needs in this arena. There is one student who will be required to sit apart from fellow students during this lesson. He is less distracted and less distractible when he is physically separated. (See above evaluation assessment.) Other students will be observed and moved if unexpected behaviors occur.

**Figure 2.7** Butterfly lesson prerequisites

expectations. Figure 2.8 shows an example from an anti-bullying lesson which reports the *findings* of the survey on prerequisite skills and learner characteristics.

Thus we see a wide variety of different approaches to the question of learner characteristics and prerequisite skills. There is clearly no one right answer to any of these steps, but rather lots of different ways to approach it depending on the topic, context, goals, objectives, test items, learners, and so forth.

### SUMMARY OF MY FINDINGS ON STUDENTS' CHARACTERISTICS

* The class consists of 12 students who have recently finished kindergarten and will be entering 1st grade.
* The class will be attending a vacation Bible school for one week in July at St. James Parish in Sewickley, PA.
* One of the students attended kindergarten at St. James School.
* One student attended kindergarten at Bon Meade Elementary School in Moon Area School district.
* One student attended kindergarten at Sewickley Academy.
* One student is currently being home schooled.
* Seven of the students attended kindergarten at Edgeworth and Osborne Elementary Schools, part of the Quaker Valley School district.
* None of these students have IEPs, or are identified with special needs.
* All of these students have received instruction in morality as part of their religious education experience, helping to shape the proper attitudes about how to treat other people.
* I was unable to obtain any information from these institutions regarding their anti-bullying curriculum. Due to the fact that the students are coming from a bunch of different schools, I suspect there will be some discrepancies in the prior knowledge. In order to assess if the students have the necessary prerequisites, I will administer a pre-test. I will ask students to describe bullying in their own words. I will ask students to identify different types of bullying (i.e., hitting, name-calling, leaving out, cyber bullying). After all 12 of the students have taken the pre-test, I will analyze the results. If students score lower than 90%, I will provide instruction regarding the prerequisites at the beginning of the lesson.
* In order to assess what learning styles my students prefer, I will have the students take a learning styles inventory, and I will ask the parents to email me the results.

**Figure 2.8** Anti-bullying lesson prerequisites

### STEP 5 Analysis of Available Texts

It is a very important step in this process to look at a variety of available texts and determine which one(s) may be useful to you in your lesson. This must come before the selection of activities or media and is a separate sort of task with a different set of criteria. There are many different guidelines out there available as checklists if you want to spend more time selecting texts. But for most of us, as very busy classroom teachers, there won't be much time to analyze texts for use in individual lessons or even for an entire class. It's easy to be handed materials and assume that they will serve the classroom needs well and then allow those very texts to drive the instruction.

---

 TEXT SELECTION COMMON ERROR
Allowing texts to drive the instruction

---

Accepting the texts and having them prescribe the learning goals and objectives—right down to the very scripts that teachers are to say—is not what instructional design is about. We all make assumptions about the instruction from the outset. Part of the most important gifts that ID will give you is the ability to look afresh at instructional moments and think them through in ways that you have not thought about them before. If you make assumptions in terms of media, activities, or texts—the three most common sets of assumptions to make—then you are short-circuiting the ID process in really harmful ways. To create the very best instruction, suspend your assumptions and focus on the instruction with as much clarity and lack of prejudice as possible.

---

 TEXT SELECTION HEURISTIC
Suspend your assumptions about texts, media, and activities choices as long as you possibly can. Focus on the learning goal as you select your texts.

---

While there are many guidelines available as mentioned before, for me it is pretty easy to boil these down to just a few primary criteria that make a text really useful. *Answering the following questions will help to make sense of which texts are useful.* Don't rely only on the texts that are given to you, or ones that you have always used, or have been recommended by others. Take the time to research resources from the library, online, or trade journals to find the best sources of information on the topic. Spend the time identifying the breadth of possibilities rather than getting mired in a single source until you're sure which one makes the most sense. Once you have assembled the texts, it's actually a relatively simple matter to look at them and assess their worth for your instruction using the following questions:

1. Does the text support my instructional goal/objectives? How closely?
2. Is the text accurate?
3. Is the text current?
4. Is the text in any way objectionable?
5. What is the "hidden curriculum" in the text? Is it acceptable?
6. Is the text exceptionally engaging or motivating?
7. Are there some really great features that I want for my instruction?

Those seven questions can pretty well identify which text you'll use. You may find one of the other checklists works better for you, or you may feel that within your particular content area you want to add questions to the list. That's fine. Customize it so that it will work well for you!

First and foremost *it is essential that you determine the extent to which the text supports your goal.* If it really doesn't but it's just the text you always use, start looking for something else. Take the time to make sure that the text is teaching the content in a way that is in clear alignment with your goals and objectives. For example, if you are teaching mathematics word problems and your learning goal is to enable children to identify word clues, but the text does not address word clues at all, then this isn't a good match. A word of caution here: You do not want to start jumping ahead of yourself by either thinking about the activities you'll use to see if the text supports those, or thinking about the media choices you *may* make and choosing a text supportive of those. No, here it is important to rely heavily on the text that will support your learning goal.

Next you'll look at a couple of relatively easy check items. Is the text *accurate*? That's easily assessed by reading it once. As an expert in the area, it will be a simple and quick matter to determine the accuracy of a text and you shouldn't spend a great deal of time examining texts for this criterion. If a text doesn't pass the accuracy test, off it goes—it's no longer on the list, even if another teacher swears by it.

Is it *current*? Most of the time a quick check of the publication date can help here, but once in a while you'll find a good text with very close alignment and discover it's unfortunately more than a decade old. Now what? Well, if the text still seems perfect and is otherwise worthy, keep it on the list, and check very carefully to make sure that the content *you'll* be using doesn't have any outdated or grossly incorrect passages.

Next, is the text in any way *objectionable*? Now here there could be many issues: Does the text portray a minority in an inappropriate way? Is there a presentation in the text of something that recently has come to be considered in different ways than is presented in the text? Are there social issues that are dealt with in a way that may seem inappropriate to some audiences? This is a harder call because too often *we* don't find something objectionable, but others do, and making ourselves highly empathetic toward others and putting ourselves in their shoes can be difficult. Often we may feel someone is overly sensitive and that something probably shouldn't bother them. However, if you think there is even a chance that someone might be offended, to the trash bin it goes. Listen to the small quiet intuitive voice that tells you this isn't the one. Likewise, try to uncover the "hidden curriculum" that may be inherent in the text. What values does the text express, what kinds of attitudes and principles are just under the surface of the formal curriculum in the book? When you look at a possible text, you have to examine the whole book including the hidden curriculum.

It's OK for you to be subjective about this choice. Books are like friends, you can love them as if they are dear to you. Don't deny yourself that, simply because there must be more objective reasons to adopt a different text for a given instructional moment. Allow yourself to look at the text and determine if it is *exceptionally engaging or motivating.* If you think it is, and particularly if you suspect your learners will feel likewise, grab it while you have it in your hot little hands.

We can array this decision making in a fairly simple chart as shown in Figure 2.9.

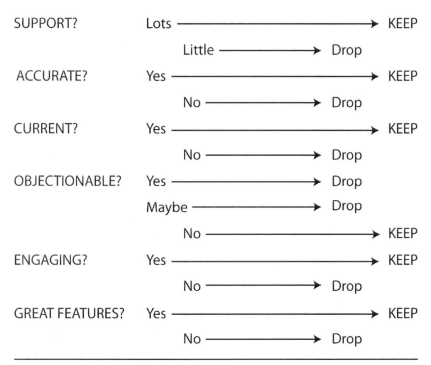

**Figure 2.9** Text selection decision-making chart

*Samples* If we return to our baseball example we see how text selection can take place even when the designer first believes that there are simply no texts for his or her content. It's pretty common to resist looking at new texts whether because you're comfortable with the one assigned, feel constrained by district requirements, or assume that your content does not lend itself to texts at all, such as physical education.

In this baseball example, the *text selection* can follow any number of a set of different questions that can be ranked or answered "yes" or "no." The initial response was similar to what many teachers of non-traditional subjects often fall into: "There are no texts for teaching *this* ..." Hats off to one instructional designer who persevered and found several texts to examine. He displayed his information in a chart as shown in Table 2.5.

This is a good start, but a few things would strengthen it. First, it is often more useful to array several text choices side by side with one another as it helps to see at a glance which ones have which benefits. Also, giving a score rather than a yes/no answer gives a clearer picture and more chance to give texts various relative advantages—it's more shades of gray. Thus the chart shown in Table 2.6 might be a better way to array this information. This again displays more information more quickly. It would be nice, if working online, to allow for links to further information keyed off of each score to explain that score, as more goes into that little number than the number would tell, and we might find this information key when making other text decisions.

Another example is from a course on world history (see Table 2.7). In the chart shown in Table 2.8 the designer has nicely considered the options side by side, but the "yes/no" options tend to oversimplify, and

**Table 2.5** Baseball text selection chart

| TEXT SELECTION CHART | | |
|---|---|---|
| Title | *Softball Skills and Drill* | *Play Better Baseball* |
| Author: | Judi Garman | Bob Cluck |
| Copyright date: | 2001 | 1994 |
| Publisher: | Human Kinetics | Contemporary Books |
| Content: | | |
| 1. Is the content accurate? Is information factually stated? | Yes | Yes |
| 2. Is the content up to date? Is the copyright date in the last 5 years? | No | No |
| 3. Is the content comprehensive? Is the content congruent with specific district with state curriculum guidelines? | Yes | Yes |
| 4. Are the social issues treated fairly? Are ethnic groups, males, and females shown in non-stereotyped roles through words and pictures? | Yes* | Yes |

* But pictures are all female as it is meant for female softball players.

**Table 2.6**  Improved baseball text selection chart

| CRITERIA | SCORE TEXT 1 | SCORE TEXT 2 | SCORE TEXT 3 | COMMENTS |
|---|---|---|---|---|
| Accurate | 4 (out of 5) | 3 | 3 | None are excellent |
| Factual | 4 | 3 | 3 | Facts could be presented more dispassionately in all three texts |
| Up to date? | 5 | 5 | 5 | All are excellent in this category |
| Copyright date? | 5 | 5 | 5 | All are current |
| Comprehensive | 5 | 4 | 3 | Text 3 is unacceptable |

**Table 2.7**  *World history* text identification chart

| | TEXTS |
|---|---|
| Primary source 1 | Textbook: *World cultures: a global mosaic* (Prentice Hall) |
| Primary source 2 | Textbook: *World history* presented by Discovery School (Prentice Hall) |
| Primary source 3 | Textbook: *World history* presented by National Geographic (Glencoe) |
| Supplementary source 1 | www.pbs.org/wnet/africa/photoscope/photoscope_aids.html |
| Supplementary source 2 | www.avert.org/aidsinafrica.htm |

**Table 2.8**  *World history* text selection chart

| QUESTIONS | PRIMARY SOURCE 1 | PRIMARY SOURCE 2 | PRIMARY SOURCE 3 | SECONDARY SOURCE 1 | SECONDARY SOURCE 2 |
|---|---|---|---|---|---|
| 1. Is the content accurate? | Yes | Yes | Yes | Yes | Yes |
| 2. Is the content up-to-date? | No | Yes | Yes | Yes | Yes |
| 3. Is the content comprehensive? | Yes | Yes` | Yes | No | No |
| 4. Are social issues treated fairly? | Yes | Yes | Yes | No | Yes |
| 5. Does the text format help make learning easy? | Yes | No | Yes | No | Yes |
| 6. Is the content presented at the appropriate grade level of learners? | Yes | Yes | Yes | Yes | No |
| 7. Does the writing style help make learning easy? | Yes | Yes | No | No | No |
| 8. Are the instructional components congruent? | Yes | No | Yes | Yes | Yes |
| 9. Do the instructional characteristics facilitate learning? | Yes | No | Yes | No | No |
| 10. Are the materials effective with students? | No | No | No | No | No |
| 11. Is use of the instructional materials compatible with the teaching conditions? | Yes | Yes | Yes | Yes | Yes |
| 12. Do the supplementary print materials help make learning easier? | Yes | Yes | Yes | No | No |

**Table 2.9** *World history* text synopsis chart

| | FINAL DETERMINATIONS |
|---|---|
| Primary source 1 | I would use *World cultures: a global mosaic* because it meets the presentation and instructional design criteria along with most of the sub-questions for each criterion. |
| Primary source 2 | I would not use *World history* presented by Discovery School because it only successfully meets the criteria for content. |
| Primary source 3 | I would consider using *World history* presented by National Geographic (Glencoe) because it meets the criteria for content and instructional design along with having astounding graphs, pictures, and charts. |
| Supplementary source 1 | I would not use www.pbs.org/wnet/africa/photoscope/photoscope_aids. html because it meets less than half of the criteria for selecting text. |
| Supplementary source 2 | I would not use www.avert.org/aidsinafrica.htm because it meets less than half of the criteria for selecting text. |

it might be stronger if we included a score rather than a dichotomous "yes/no" option. The conclusion (see Table 2.9, above) indicates which texts were selected and why, and is a very important addition to the design document.

### STEP 6  Create and Specify Learning Activities

This is one of the favorite steps for most of us. At this moment we can be really creative—well, within some logical limits at least. The activities are the meat of what you do in the instructional moment. Here is where you have the opportunity to really think about what activities will be well matched to the goals and objectives for your instruction. What activities will help your learner manage the test items you've designed? Be cautious, don't just decide to do something because it would be fun, make sure the fun stuff is aligned, that's the watchword. The most important rule here is to keep your head about you and not create activities that are not really targeted at the instructional goal or that are mismatches with your learners, text, or objectives. Too often we say, "Oh it would be fun to do a roleplay," or "Let's ditch the lecture and do a case study instead" when what is really called for in the instruction is a good old-fashioned lecture—or a roleplay might be fun, but not help the learner to meet the goals of the instruction.

It is important at this point to remind you that we are not talking about *media* here. Media are the *ways* that we carry our message into the instruction, so media are things like videos, film strips, and computer learning environments of all types. It's easy to become confused though, because, for example, a game is more of an activity if it's carried out via computer. A video game, then, is *both* a media and an activity choice within a single decision. It is important to pull these apart and separate the choices. First, determine what activities you want (gaming) and *then* decide about the media (via computer, small groups face-to-face, board game, video, etc.).

**ACTIVITY SPECIFICATION COMMON ERROR**
Confusing activities and media

There are extensive lists of activities and this is one of the places where we can rely heavily on recent research and theory about what helps learners reach different types of goals effectively. For example, learning to swim is rarely best accomplished through a lecture, and most of the research in kinesiology will support the notion of repeated physical practice with effective modeling, demonstration, and timely feedback. These are the activities that will effectively support the learning of what we call a psychomotor skill. Now the model we are using here tends toward more behavioral outcomes, by focusing on the goal. However, it is perfectly acceptable—and many times it is appropriate—to also consider much more open models of learning such as problem-based learning or constructivist learning.

There is an almost endless list of classroom activities which can be sensibly categorized into more or less active learning. There are a large number of taxonomies of learning activities that are divided not only based on active versus passive ones, but also into learning theories or learning style, classroom type, teacher preferences, and so forth. Naturally, a particular activity such as problem-based case-solving *could* be employed in a classroom in a very behavioral fashion, but it wouldn't be common because those two don't really match up well. Many theorists have created very complicated algorithms to make these choices more straightforward. There have even been attempts to create an "ID in the box" meant to help make such ID decisions more or less automatically. I would argue that it's almost impossible to do this despite our best knowledge of research informing our decisions. It's a creative act, and one that needs to have the individual teacher at the center of the decision making. Doing ID and particularly aligning proper activities with all the prior pieces of an ID process is as much art as it is science. Computers are great for some things, but making this level of ID decision is probably best left to real teachers doing the real work of education.

Most ID experts agree that an instructional strategy or activity should have the following five components: *pre-instructional activities* such as setting motivation, attention, sharing objectives with the learners, and establishing prerequisite learning; *information presentation* including the stimulus materials, where most of the content is shared in whatever form and through whatever activities make the most sense in terms of alignment with the instruction; *student participation* which would include guidance of the learners as they engage the materials, performance, and feedback; *testing* in which the learning is assessed; and *follow-through* for both retention and transfer.

Arguments can certainly be mounted about whether any categorization works in all cases, but what remains critical is a careful consideration while selecting learning activities rather than simply selecting among your favorites, or most comfortable, or newest ideas. There are some research findings that have been established through the years that are worth considering as you design your learning activities. Among these are that people learn at different paces and in different ways, that learners enter the classroom with different expectations and with different entry level skills, and even with different levels of motivation. This knowledge mostly leads us to use a *variety* of different activities to try to meet the learners where they are.

As a way to start you thinking about how to best match up your activities with your goals, objectives and test items, here are a few guidelines adapted from Madhumita & Kumar's 1995 work:

- Motivate the learner with relevance. Make sure that the materials you give the learner will be interesting by finding out what is relevant to their lives. Many a poignant story is told about the cultural mismatch between students and teachers from very different cultural backgrounds. So make sure you know who your learners are and how to motivate them.

- Match the level of instructional activity and learning to the level of learner reception. That is, we know there is a "zone of proximal development" (Vygotsky, 1978) in which the learner is sufficiently challenged to keep their interests but they are not struggling so mightily that they are frustrated. We often say we're "in the zone"—that's what we're talking about here. Try hard to identify activities that will challenge but not frustrate the learner.

- Offer advance organizers that will let the learner know what is coming in the lesson and may serve as a scaffold to their development.

- Divide up complex tasks into smaller chunks that will help to build satisfaction and confidence in the learners.

- Help learners to make sense of the learning through graphic organizers when you can.

- Organize complicated information into easy-to-remember structures such as mnemonics or graphics.

- Vary activities for increased sustained interest and motivation.

- Assess the learner's understanding with questions and answers.

- Ensure the learning environment is as much like the performance environment as possible. Thus, if the test will happen in a classroom, the learning may make sense in a classroom, but if the testing is going to be on a shop floor, then the instruction should be on a shop floor whenever feasible.

- Use the mastery learning model in which learners are aiming at a specific outcome or learning goal that has been pre-defined. Mastery learning does not rank order people or give them the same kinds of grades, rather they pass or fail the specific task.

- Engage the learners in active learning as much as possible.

- Use different strategies in an effort to encourage metacognition (thinking about their thinking).

- Try to vary your approach, even in one lesson, to reach different learning styles.

- Provide immediate feedback to learners' responses.

- Prepare extension, enrichment, and self-learning exercises to allow the learner more opportunities to master the materials, perhaps on their own.
- Make sure to sum up your lesson with a conclusion that highlights the main points covered in the session.

ACTIVITY SPECIFICATION HEURISTIC
Many activities are available to you so select the one(s) that best align with your instruction including the goal, objectives, and test items

Thus, within these guidelines you can choose almost any activities that apply to your situation, that make sense given the content. If you're teaching map-reading skills, perhaps a field trip makes sense. If you're teaching about wine tasting, make sure the learning environment is similar to the kind of place where you'd hope the learners would display their skills in the future (a party atmosphere might make sense). If you're working out how to use software, you'd better engage the learners with a computer in a way that provides relevance and active learning as much as possible. So certain guidelines will make more sense than others depending on your situation. You are all highly skilled professionals, or will be if you're still in a preparation program, and so this text need not give more than just these guidelines that you can apply. It is not for me or anyone else, in my view, to try to prescribe the proper instructional activities for a given situation. In fact, doing so will tend to de-professionalize being a teacher. You know what your classroom is like, you know your goal, and so you know what needs to be done. If you are preparing to be a teacher, you will gain confidence as you spend time in your classroom or classrooms that will be like your future classroom. In this process you will also have clarity about what your learners need, what you can use to best effect for your own future classroom. The next step is to begin to figure out which activities you'll use and then what media will support those activities.

*Samples* Activities are the first place where charts almost always make sense and you're not likely to be able to really show the flow of all the components without arraying them in a chart. The selection of activities must be aligned nicely with the goals and assessments and all the prior steps to this point, which feed into this fun and innovative step in the process.

In Table 2.10 (below), I'm starting at a mid-point in the baseball plan so as to show the nature of the "meat" of the lesson. Here we have three steps that are being described. I'd like to see more detail in this description. The materials development will offer an opportunity to see the precise pictures and video. Instruction and demonstration seem like the right way to characterize what's happening, but the content is not really fleshed out here. The notion behind this level of planning is that a substitute teacher might be able to come into the class, use this as their starting point, and teach the lesson because there is sufficient detail for them to do so.

The butterfly lesson activity shown in Figure 2.10 is really well done, particularly in the level of detail. A substitute teacher could easily pick this up and figure out what to do when. There are a few issues, however. First, the work could be better laid out in a chart rather than an open document which might help in terms of readability. Also, there is a problem with some of the specificity, thus we do not know for sure what a "student-friendly" manner is, for example. More concerning than these minor issues is the very common tendency to

**Table 2.10** Baseball activities excerpt chart

| | | |
|---|---|---|
| 3. Prerequisites | Assume catching a thrown ball, verbal articulation, and knowledge of left and right. | Teacher's instruction |
| 4. Information and examples | Provide pictures of proper positioning next to the base. Provide video or step-by-step pictures of moving from defensive position to correct receiving position. | Teacher's instruction and demonstration |
| 5. Practice and feedback | Run through the instruction as a group so as to better understand the characteristics of the players. Then group the players so they represent mixed ability. Then have players move into the correct receiving position. The players receive the ball correctly, players move off of base correctly, and I move to each group and provide feedback. | Teacher's instruction and students' practice |
| 6. Testing | Give individual assessment, consisting of nine items with up to five iterations for each item. | Teacher's instruction and students' execution |

1. **Motivation:** Observe and discuss one stage of butterfly lifecycle pupa *(specimen, teacher)*
   - Ask students what they think the specimen is. Allow time for silly/nonsensical answers; this helps to engage students.
   - Begin to ask explicit questions "Can anyone tell me what a baby butterfly looks like?"
   - Explain that kittens look like cats, but baby butterflies do not look like adult butterflies.
   - Tell them that the object you are holding is one step, or stage, in the butterfly's life. (It is necessary to move around the room during the questioning/discussion time, so that all students get a chance to see the pupa.)
2. **Objectives:** Tell students they will learn about the butterfly lifecycle
   - Teacher will read the lesson's objectives in a student-friendly manner. (Make it sound fun, not clinical.)
3. **Prerequisites:** Vocabulary: assumes the ability to sequence *(journal, teacher)*. Assumes little, if any, unease with subject matter
   - Each of the eight words will be laminated and printed on orange stock (color-coded for science).
   - Teacher will hold a word up and ask for a student volunteer to read it. The class will repeat the word.
   - Ask for a volunteer to define the word: "Does anyone know what a caterpillar is?"
   - Teacher will clarify the definition: "A caterpillar, also called a larva, is the 2nd stage in a butterfly's lifecycle."
   - Students will use their own words and drawings to record meaning in their science journals.
     Choose a student name from the "cup of fate" to determine who hangs the word onto the word wall.
     Introduce each word in this manner. Teacher will keep a deliberate pace to this part of the lesson; students will be reminded that overly-detailed images are not appropriate in this part of science.
   - Move around the room, assess progress of the ELL and Title I students. Offer help, if necessary. *(Vocabulary—egg, adult, caterpillar, chrysalis, larva, pupa, lifecycle, butterfly)*
   - Model behavior towards subject matter you would like students to adopt acceptance and interest.
4. **Information and examples:** Explains stages and sequence of lifecycle textbook *(whiteboard, teacher)*
   - Have students turn to p. 8 in *The life cycle of a butterfly*. Set a purpose for reading (PFR): "Our PFR is to find out how many stages there are in the butterfly's lifecycle."
   - Ask student volunteers to read in their best "teacher's voice."
   - Help students summarize the content. Ask, "How many stages are there? What are the names of the stages?" See lifecycle diagram, p. 9.
     Discuss the diagram and the meaning of the arrows (start at the egg stage).
   - Use the PowerPoint file on the interactive whiteboard. The PP file contains close-up photographs and video of the Monarch lifecycle.
   - Explicitly teach the 4 stages, using correct vocabulary and pointing out identifying features of each stage.
5. **Practice and feedback:** Class T/F quiz *(whiteboard and diagram, labsheet, inflatable props)*
   - Teacher will show (previously hidden) large inflatable butterfly props *(labsheet, teacher)*

- Beginning with the egg, hold up and ask students to "group shout" the name of this butterfly stage; hold up inflatable caterpillar and ask for another "group shout" of the name; proceed same steps with chrysalis and butterfly. Informally assess answers.
- Feedback: class repeats "oh yeah!" after teacher (energizer that lets students "celebrate" correct answers).
- Tell students we're going to answer some questions on our quest to become junior lepidopterists (define term) using the "popcorn" method. Throw the egg to a student, read the 1st question from whiteboard and student answers.
- Ask the class to give a thumbs-up/thumbs-down if they agree/disagree with the answer. Informally assess answers.
- Feedback will include silent cheers, clam claps, and other "energizers" when they answer correctly.
- Students will be given a 2-sided labsheet; they will complete the practice diagram by labeling and numbering the stages that are shown. Upon completion, I will assess their sheets for accuracy and affix a butterfly sticker.
- The back side is a "Junior Lepidopterist" certificate. Write their name upon correct completion on the front side and ask them to color the butterfly border while they wait for their classmates to finish.

6. **Testing:** lifecycle project: draw, sequence, and label lifecycle stages *(four-square worksheet)*
- Teacher will read the directions to complete the assessment.
- Teacher will model the steps necessary to complete the worksheet project.
- All supplies will be readily available (scissors, pencils, gluestick, construction paper).
- Teacher-made model will be shown and hung on whiteboard (sans assessed information).
- Leveled readers about butterflies will be available for early finishers.
  - Group 1: *Born to be a butterfly*
  - Group 2: *From caterpillar to butterfly*
  - Group 3: *How and why: insects grow and change*
  - Group 4: *A true book: insects*

7. **Enrichment and remediation** *(computer software)*
- Remediation will be through computer software that reviews the stages of the lifecycle and then offers practice by having the learner put them in order.
- Graded feedback is immediate.
- Enrichment is through BrainPop computer software—*Metamorphosis* video. This animated video will extend the learners' understanding of which creatures go through different kinds of metamorphosis, plus the difference between complete and incomplete metamorphosis.

**Figure 2.10** Butterfly lesson activities

specify the media at this stage, in the form of videos and Power-Point presentation. The activity should specify "presentation" by the teacher or lecturer, and the media for delivering that lecture, be it PowerPoint, overheads, or blackboard, and should not be selected at the activities step.

### STEP 7  Selecting Media

Media selection is one of the most slippery decisions made in the instructional design process. This is because most of us come to the process of creating instruction with an idea in mind of what our classroom looks like. And even if we're unsure about which activities we'll use, what approaches we'll employ, we all too often have a clear image of what media we'll use to convey the content. We may have a favorite medium, or perhaps we have a comfort level with PowerPoint that far outstrips our comfort level with interactive whiteboards (like SMART boards). For many reasons, media selection is a prime example of a place where most instructional decisions fall out of alignment with the overall thrust of the instructional design up to that point.

It's hard to say why our imaginations are so captured by media and new technologies. It's quite possible that we're enchanted by them, or that we see our students as enchanted by them. They're "cool" and

**Figure 2.11** Technology-focused learning. Photo by Jules Carr-Chellman.

"glitzy." We focus on the ways in which media can motivate rather than the ways in which media can support the instruction—that feels a little mundane. There are many factors to consider when selecting media for your lesson. Among the big categories are the characteristics of the media, characteristics of your learners, characteristics of the task/learning, learning environment, development environment, economy, culture, and practical factors.

We can look at each of these briefly as we consider a given medium. For example, let's think of a class on addition in the 1st grade. There are a number of possible media for this including a computer game, a board game (note that "game" would be the activity rather than the medium, the way it's delivered then would be the medium), blackboard, SMART board, overhead projector, and naturally math manipulatives are an option. We might first look at the *characteristics of the media* so we have a clear understanding of each of these. Some, for example, need electricity; others do not, these are just the characteristics of the media. Then we'd consider the learner characteristics, some of which we may know from our analysis of prerequisite skills. Perhaps they do not yet know how to work a computer, or they are learning that. Perhaps they are not captured by computer games, but board games are interesting to them. Perhaps there has been a history of frustration with the SMART board in the past, or fear and trembling when approaching the chalkboard.

We would then look at the *task characteristics*. And this is vital. We need, here, to make sense of what it is we're asking the learner to do. Are we having them practice? Are they learning new content? Are they conceptually breaking down addition? Does what we're asking them to do align with the medium we select? What is the *learning environment* like? Do we have electricity?—don't laugh, plenty in Nepal do not! Are computers at the ready and are there support folks who make things go smoothly when the computer is cantankerous? Is there a SMART board or a chalkboard? Where is it located in the room? Are the desks arranged so that everyone can see it? Is there too much light in the room at that time of day to consider an overhead projector?

What is the *development environment* like? Mostly this is going to be either your classroom, your house, or your teacher's lounge. Perhaps there's a lab in your school where you can go to create PowerPoint presentations or other multimedia solutions, but in most cases it's going to be a space where you are working on your own. So consider that space: Do you have access at home—where you do most of your planning—to create an online solution? Do you have access in your classroom to search for addition games online? These are all crucial elements of the development environment that you should take into consideration when selecting a medium.

The *economy and the culture* as well as practical factors are also essential elements of smart media decision making. Will the culture accept this particular medium or will it be foreign to them, potentially offensive, or even a source of ridicule for you or the learners? That may sound far-fetched, but in some cultures even the use of a computer is something that is beyond appropriate for the indigenous group. Does the school have the money to purchase what is needed? Is there a less expensive solution that will work? Are there pressures to use the new technology? Perhaps it was recently purchased and/or costly and so using something at a higher level may serve a political purpose?

In all of these considerations there are generally thought to be two levels or stages of choice for an instructional medium. *The first stage is focused on effective communication to the learner of the content and objectives.* Here we are concerned primarily with the media, learner, and task characteristics. During this stage we would ask questions such as: What content are we covering in this lesson? What information do the learners need to receive to meet the objectives? What types of activities must the learner do to engage in the learning?

*The second stage is thought of as acceptance in which we're focused on the cost, environment, culture, human factors, and other practical considerations.* Here we are more likely to be concerned with the learning and development environment, the economy and culture, and other practical factors. We would ask questions during this stage such as: Will the classroom and school support this? Will my colleagues, administration, and parents support this choice? Is it too costly? Will it work?

Alex Romiszowski has a wonderful "wheel" approach to deciding about media selection. Based on his work (Romiszowski, 1981) I've created a similar wheel for the classroom media selection process (see Figure 2.12).

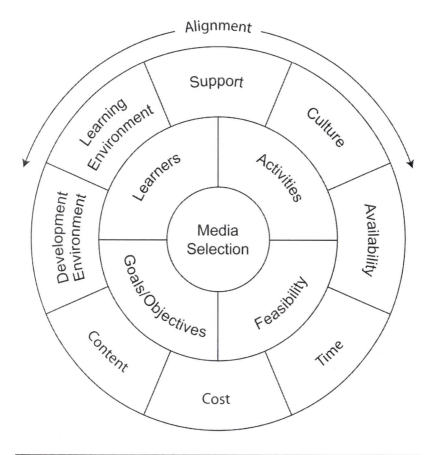

**Figure 2.12** Teacher media selection wheel

Ultimately, the selection of a medium for your lesson will make sense as you place it into the context of the entire process of ID. *If you came into the experience planning a certain medium for use, then you've missed a huge chunk of what ID can offer you.*

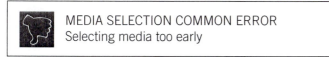

MEDIA SELECTION COMMON ERROR
Selecting media too early

The entire process is short-circuited when it is planned that the lesson will be "a PowerPoint lesson." I hear this frequently, and we see it very often in requests for instructional designers to create some instruction. The idea that the medium is already set before any ID has happened is almost as common as Starbucks outlets or reality TV shows. It is imperative that you put the media choices off until it is appropriate and you have a clear picture of the goals, objectives, tests, and so forth.

*Sample* Returning to our example of computer building, our instructional designer has created a good chart that compares media forms (Table 2.11). There are a number of different criteria that can be used to determine the best media, although alignment always trumps them all. Matching with the activities is perhaps the most important connection to determine which medium makes the most sense. In this way I really like this chart because it brings in the activities twice, once with an assessment and once with a reminder of what the activity is.

**STEP 8  Planning for Implementation and Trying It Out**

Implementing instruction is one of the most exciting and exhausting parts of any ID process. Here we're going to try it out with a group of learners. If you can find a group of learners who are *not* actually in your proposed class, but are as close to them as possible, that's ideal. By this I mean that if you teach high school and can round up some students from the neighborhood or try it out on your own kids, that's fine. Better that than trying it out on your spouse who is really not particularly close to the target age and demographic.

There are typically three types of trials, and most of us will never go through all three levels, but in ID circles we understand the one-on-one trial, the small group trial, and the large group trial as being three levels of attempts to see how the instruction works in the "real world." It is definitely the case, and I can tell you this from experience, that when I go through all three of these levels, I am able to learn a *lot* more than if I only go through one, particularly if it's just the one-on-one trial. I never applied that level of implementation in a classroom setting, but did so when I used ID in a corporate setting where there

**Table 2.11** Computer build media selection chart

| MEDIUM | PRACTICALITY | APPROPRIATENESS | FIT WITH INSTRUCTIONAL ACTIVITIES | INSTRUCTIONAL ACTIVITY |
|---|---|---|---|---|
| PowerPoint presentation | My classroom is already equipped with a computer and projector so PowerPoint is a great way for me to display information. Because of the availability, there is no extra cost for using this medium. | This is a very appropriate medium for the classroom. I would display information for all students to see, and they are all very comfortable with viewing information in this way. | This medium fits in very well with my activity. I would use this to display information such as the objectives for the class period and the steps I need the students to follow for certain activities. Because it is displayed, it is a great way to inform students and it is large to catch their attention. | Display objectives Prerequisite practice and feedback |
| SMART Sympodium | My classroom is already equipped with a sympodium so no extra cost would be incurred. This medium is used often and was designed for the classroom setting. | The students have become accustomed to using a sympodium in the classroom. The students get excited to use this medium because it allows them to interact with the displayed material. | This medium will be used for students to label displayed graphics. This definitely gains their attention and most students are excited to come and write on it. | Prerequisite |
| Computers | My classroom is already equipped with computers for building purposes for every student. The students have grown up using this medium and are always willing and excited to use it. | This medium is very appropriate for my instructional unit. It will be a great tool in order to demonstrate the steps and tasks the students will be expected to achieve. Regular classroom computers will be used to assist the PowerPoint presentations and use of the sympodium. | This fits well with the instructional activity because the activity is about computers. The students will be using computers and their parts to build a functioning computer. Once built, students will use the computers to accomplish different tasks. | Motivation Practice and feedback Testing Enrichment and remediation |

*(continued)*

**Table 2.11** Continued

| MEDIUM | PRACTICALITY | APPROPRIATENESS | FIT WITH INSTRUCTIONAL ACTIVITIES | INSTRUCTIONAL ACTIVITY |
|---|---|---|---|---|
| Video: www.youtube.com/watch?v=zy–YUTuuh7zo | The use of a YouTube video is a great medium to display information or gain examples. The computer and the internet are already provided so there is no extra cost. Because of the nature of the video, it fits nicely into this educational setting. | This medium is very appropriate for this age group of students (high school). Most students use this site for their own entertainment, so using this in an educational setting always grabs their attention. This video breaks down an example of what the students will be doing within their build project. | This medium fits with the activity. The video shows an individual installing a hard drive the same way the students will. I would use this video to reinforce the demonstration that I would provide the students. | Information and examples |
| Demonstration (face-to-face instruction) | The use of demonstration is extremely practical for this unit. The students will be completing a motor skill activity. There is no cost involved as the teacher is using the appropriate computer equipment provided. | The use of demonstration as a medium is very appropriate for this type of unit. The students are gaining a motor skill of connecting and placing components. There is no better way for students to learn than to watch a demonstration in action. Because of the nature of demonstration, especially with computer components, the students will stay attentive. | This medium is very appropriate with this activity. Because the students are gaining a motor skill, demonstration is the best way to learn. The teacher would be able to use the computer components and cables to show how they are placed and connected. | Information and examples |

are more luxuries of time and sometimes a different need to be precise about outcomes (such as flying airplanes and other high-risk training). For the purposes of ID in the K-12 classroom, it's best to consider simply doing a small group trial with a population as close to the target as can be found—and perhaps bribed with cupcakes.

Once you have completed your trials, you're ready for prime time! How will you implement the final instruction? Can you see any resistors that are likely to hold you back, e.g., people, resources, or system wide? Start thinking about all of the supports that you may need to help you overcome any likely resistance to effective implementation.

 IMPLEMENTATION COMMON ERROR
Assuming all will go as planned with little or no resistance

It can be hard to imagine that when you have spent a great deal of time working through the design process and created what you think is a fantastic celebration of American quilts, or the perfect approach to the difficult intricacies of polynomials, perhaps it may not go as planned. Trying it out is a first step but you should also prepare yourself for the needs of the larger group that you'll work with in reality and know that there may be resistance when the instructional design goes into a larger-scale implementation. Perhaps the parents will complain because they don't like the new approach, or the administration may object if the process is more costly or time-consuming, or if it is hearing from parents or other community factions. There are so many possible obstacles out there waiting to disrupt the well-laid plans you've crafted. So be prepared for them, have a "Plan B." Anticipate what you can because the unexpected may still hit and could derail your lesson if you're not prepared to be flexible and proactive.

 IMPLEMENTATION HEURISTIC
Have a "Plan B," expect the unexpected, and remain flexible

One implementation tool many people find very useful is a *force field analysis*. Here you can begin to break out the forces for and against the effective implementation. For example, forces *for* might include availability of technology, funds to create materials, and political support for the use of problem-based learning approaches. Forces *against* might be lack of funds for materials creation, poor lighting in the room, and parents unwilling to accept new learning approaches. Naturally, these various forces for and against are probably going to be stronger or weaker depending largely on things like proximity to the issue, stakeholder role, inflexibility of the force, and so forth. We can show these in a graphic (see Figure 2.13).

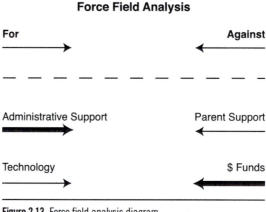

**Figure 2.13** Force field analysis diagram

*Sample* Let's take a look back at our butterfly example for a good approach to arraying the needed information for the implementation plan (see Table 2.12).

Completing this implementation plan was similar to the mental and written checklists that I do for my lessons already. I have been accused of being as organized as a drill sergeant, both at home and school, so this type of preparation seems just a bit beyond what I would do naturally. I can't imagine running through this chart for every lesson that I would teach at the elementary level each day, but it certainly would help keep order for the beginning of units since much of the supports, materials, and assessments would be the same. The funny thing is, no matter how thoroughly we plan for those things that could go wrong, it's the stuff you can't prepare for that can really throw a lesson. Anyone who works with younger children will tell you

**Table 2.12** Butterfly lesson implementation plan

| OBJECTIVES | ACTIVITY | MEANS AND MEDIA | ASSESSMENT INSTRUMENT | WHO WILL DO IT? |
|---|---|---|---|---|
| 1. Without aid, students will use colored pencils and paper to illustrate the stages in the butterfly lifecycle and attain 80% mastery. | Motivation: observe/discuss one stage of butterfly lifecycle. Information: explicit instruction about the stages in the butterfly lifecycle. How many stages? What are the identifying features of each stage? | Teacher-led class discussion: questioning, clarifying, and predicting the stages. | • Informal assessment of class discussion.<br>• Lifecycle assessment illustration section scored using criteria in the rubric. | Teacher will supply specimen from personal collection. |
| 2. After being instructed to begin at the egg stage, students will sequence their illustrations into the correct stages of the organism's lifecycle with 80% mastery. | Information and prerequisite: explicit instruction about the four stages in the butterfly lifecycle. Begin at egg stage and name the stages in order. What is the stage after caterpillar called? What stage comes before the adult? | • Group-read literature about the butterfly lifecycle.<br>• Teacher lecture: PowerPoint or SMART board.<br>• Teacher demonstration: guided practice to complete lifecycle strip. | • Student journals: summarizing vocabulary.<br>• Pre-assess sequence worksheet (done the day before).<br>• Lifecycle test sequence section: scored using criteria in the rubric. | • Teacher will procure texts.<br>• Teacher will create word wall vocabulary.<br>• Teacher will assess each student's journal and formal test, and complete rubrics. |
| 3. Given a word bank, students will name each of the stages of their illustrations with 80% mastery. | Practice: names and identifying features of the 4 stages in lifecycle. | • Teacher demonstration with props.<br>• Whole group quiz via questions on a SMART board.<br>• Individual practice with labsheet. | • Lifecycle test vocabulary section: scored using criteria in the rubric.<br>• Lifecycle practice labsheet.<br>• Informal group quiz activity. | • Teacher will create PowerPoint.<br>• Teacher will model all steps to complete the project.<br>• Teacher will grade the final project.<br>• Students will be assessed individually.<br>• Teacher will collect data for informal assessment during group quiz. |

(continued)

**Table 2.12** Continued

| WHEN WILL IT HAPPEN? | WHAT SUPPORTS ARE NEEDED? | WHAT MATERIALS ARE NEEDED? | ACCOMMODATIONS /DIFFERENTIATION |
|---|---|---|---|
| • Pupa specimen shown in classroom the day before.<br>• Begin lesson with pupa. | Para-educator aid required per student IEP. | Pupa specimen; PowerPoint. | Title I and ESL students: eye contact and continued observation to ensure students are on-task. Gifted students: higher-level questions may be asked during discussion. ESL students may take assessment to itinerant teacher to complete |
| • Allow 2 weeks to borrow texts from library or team teachers.<br>• Allow 5 days to type, print and laminate word wall vocabulary.<br>• This portion of lesson to immediately follow pupa specimen. | • School librarian or 2nd grade team teachers.<br>• Copy center.<br>• Librarian to laminate words. | Supplemental text *The lifecycle of a butterfly* (1 per student; or 1 book per 2 students). Word wall vocabulary—laminated and color-coded. Student journals. Teacher-created student reference model. Lifecycle 4-square worksheet, colored pencils, erasers. Rubric per student. | Title I and ESL students: during round-robin reading, teacher will stand by their desks to offer reading suppport. Teacher will be available during assessment to redirect and answer questions that may come up.<br>Gifted students: assign harder reading passage; higher-level questions asked. |
| • Teacher will allow 3–5 days to create the file. Sequence sheet will be pulled from files 5 days before and sent to be copied (make extra copies).<br>• Teacher will have inflatable props blown up and placed out of sight on the morning of the lesson. | • Make extra copies of all worksheets and tests (5 extra copies in case of mistakes).<br>• Have phone contact information available for school IT staff in event of problem.<br>• Have back-up plan ready in case of technical problems, i.e., poster or overhead.<br>• Important to keep props out of sight until this part of the lesson to get motivation boost. | SMART board file. Inflatable props. Rubric. | Title I and ESL students: big props are visual aid to below-average learners and Title I students. Gifted students and early-finishers: leveled readers that explore the subject matter in more depth will be available for students to read. Students will be instructed what to do upon completion of assessment before they begin. Discuss similarities and differences of other creatures' lifecycles. |

about how a young child vomiting during your anticipatory set can grind things to a halt very quickly (especially when there's a sympathy vomiter in the class—ugh). Janitor with sawdust as support?

This plan is really a strong example of implementation. The designer has thought of most of the unexpected outcomes, including vomiting. I am impressed that the chart displays the most critical of those. In too many cases at this point in the process, we see a combination of media and activities charts, as though the charts were building in the same way as the process is building, but this tendency can create rather unwieldy charts that become hard for designers and users to read and use effectively. I also really like how thorough this chart is in terms of thinking through the issues that are likely to emerge (pardon the pun) in the butterfly lesson.

### STEP 9   Evaluating and Revising the Instruction

Evaluation is often simply divided into two forms based on the outcomes of evaluation activities. The first is aimed at improving, and this is called *formative evaluation*. The second is aimed at decision making and assessing effectiveness and it's called *summative evaluation*. Formative evaluation is often what most people think evaluation is all about and concerns gathering lots of data about how learners may perceive the instruction. "Smile tests" are a common form of formative evaluation; however, they are insufficient to make good revisions to the instruction. The iterative nature of ID is critical to a deep understanding of the process, which is very circular. We look carefully at the test items, for example, to discern which ones work and which ones do not. Test items that didn't work may be flawed test items, or they may point to a flaw in the instruction itself. We examine outcomes measures to see what might need to be changed in the instruction in order to improve the final outcomes.

We may also look at the outcomes data to help us make decisions about the future of an instructional unit. For example, an instructional designer may determine that a given lesson needs to be eliminated.

This sort of formative evaluation is less common in classrooms than it is in corporate ID, but it does happen. In addition, classroom teacher-designers sometimes make decisions for more than just minor adjustments that might be the result of a good formative evaluation and would require complete re-works of instructional lessons. These are all hallmarks of good evaluation.

---

EVALUATION HEURISTIC
There are two kinds of evaluation: for improvement and for decision-making

---

An evaluation plan should consider both formative and summative aspects as well as the role of stakeholders and decision-makers in the decision-making process. It may also be wise to consider the role of powerbrokers, if there are some, that are relevant to the evaluation decisions. The types of data to be collected, as well as actual data reports, if you have them, are critical to both formative and summative evaluation. At a bare minimum, a complete ID document needs to have a clear plan for data collection and an indicator of what that data will inform, in terms of formative or summative evaluation tasks, in as much detail as possible (e.g., we'll use the results of this observation to determine if the slide show worked as intended).

---

EVALUATION COMMON ERROR
Relying too heavily on informal data for evaluation

---

Too often we think that we can tell how the instruction is going through informal means, and this is a dangerous trap. Data can tell us a *very* different story from the more informal observations or assumptions made by teachers about their learners' satisfaction. Too often there is a feeling that we *know*, we know the students, we know the outcomes, we know how they feel, what they think, how they did, what they understand, and what they might have missed. We might plan to have some conversations after the session, maybe with the learners in the lunchroom or perhaps a whole-class discussion, or an individual interview with one of the students in the hallway. All of this is extremely useful information, and you know more than anyone how honest your students will be with you in different settings. However, it is important to make sure that you collect more traditional and formal data from things like brief end-of-class surveys or test item analyses. The evaluation plan should include formal and informal means of learning about the effectiveness of your lesson. Did it work? Did it fail? How do you know? Which parts were great and which needed some help? Will you repeat the lesson next year? How can you improve it? This is the part of the process where you literally go back to the start of the cycle and re-cycle back through the entire process. In order to really return to the start of the process, like an air-conditioning system in a house, you have to have some input—some fresh air—to go back into the improvement of the lesson.

The last part of the process is to make it better. As my mother used to say, "Good, better, best, never let 'em rest, till the good gets better and the better gets best!" The idea is that this process never really finishes, because your learners will change, your goals may need to change with shifting state standards or community needs, the texts become outdated, and text selection needs to be revisited from time to time. This iterative nature, where we revisit decisions every once in a while, is essential to the continuous improvement of all instruction. As I write this, I'm reviewing an old lesson I taught years ago on quilts and pioneer times. I can't even tell you how many things I'd change now, many years later, if I had the chance to go back and do that lesson again today. And if I had been refining that lesson for the last 10 years, I believe that it would now be a really robust part of the curriculum.

*Samples* Typically the revisions process moves away from the charts and tables form of display and we return to text-based presentation, which is certainly appropriate. For some designers, the charts will get a bit tedious and if you've combined the activities, media, and implementation issues, you'll be glad to move away from the charts at this point.

The first example (Figure 2.14) is actually drawn from a chemical equilibrium high school lesson, but it could probably be from almost any lesson. I'm fond of the "red light/green light" idea in this plan, but

Once the lesson has been taught, revisions will be made based on teacher observations and student responses.

A. While teaching and/or immediately after completing the lesson, I will answer the following questions based on my observations during the lesson:
  1. What were the weaknesses of the lesson?
  2. What were the strengths of the lesson?
  3. Were there any issues with the technology used?
  4. Did the class appear to understand the connections between the objectives and the lesson taught?
  5. Was the content and time frame appropriate (too much/too little time; too much/too little content)?
  6. Did the activities support the content being taught?
  7. Did the assessment used in the lesson provide adequate information about the learning?
  8. Were there points in the lesson when students were not paying attention? If so, what part of the lesson was an issue? To how many students?
  9. Were there any typos or unclear points in the presentation notes?

B. Student learning will be assessed the next day when we go over the homework assigned at the end of the lesson. I will collect their work and record the number of students that missed each problem. I will use this information to determine what information needs to be reinforced. I will then split the students into two groups, those who got at least 80% of the problems correct and those who did not. The first group will be assigned the challenge problem and the second group will receive remediation.

C. Another form of student assessment that I will take advantage of during the lesson is "red-light/green-light." At the beginning of class I give each student a red and a green index card. As I teach the lesson, I stop periodically and ask students for their "light." The idea is that if they are understanding the lesson and are ready to "go" on to the next idea, they will hold up a green card; however, if they are confused with the material, or feel like they need another example before moving on, they hold up the red card, indicating their desire to stop and slow down. Depending on the time left in the class, I have to make a judgment call on how many red cards it takes to make me stop and slow down. If there is plenty of time, I may stop for one or two students; if we are short of time, I may tell those few students concerned to come in for extra help.

D. A form of informal evaluation is done by paying attention to the number of emails I receive from students asking questions and the number of students coming in for extra help before or after school. I do not believe that a few questions indicate there is a problem with the lesson, but if a number of students appear to be confused by certain portions of the lesson, that tells me that I need to make some revisions.

E. Finally, I will use the scores on the chapter test to formally assess student performance. If there are any goals for which the test questions were missed by more than 20% of the class, I will go back and revise the lesson plan [Figure 2.13] for that goal.

**Figure 2.14** Chemical equilibrium revisions plan

might have liked just a bit more connection to the content and the entire unit.

Now we will look at the computer build lesson revision plan (Figure 2.15). I'm quite fond of the organization of this one because it divides the lesson into parts, which shows a very clear consideration of evaluation and revision throughout the entire lesson. There are, of course, many other ways of organizing that would also show clear consideration and would depend a good deal on the specifics of the lesson itself.

---

**DATA COLLECTION AND REVISION**

Throughout the entire process of creating and implementing the instructional plan for the computer build project, revision should be considered. Each step of the process may be revised to make instruction better for the next time around. In order to effectively revise the different steps of the planning process, data must be collected to make accurate decisions. Below I have stated the way I will collect data and make revisions in each phase of the process.

Pre-instruction:
*Review activity:* On the day of the instruction, another informal assessment would occur. I would have pictures of a motherboard and the back of a computer that would be labeled by the students. I would use a spinner to randomly select students to use the Sympodium to label the specific part. From this activity, I would be able to analyze the data from the correct/incorrect responses from the students and be able to revise this material for the next year. (The activity can be viewed in the "Instructional Activities" section under "prerequisites.")

*Motivational activity:* Before the instruction occurred, I would also be able to go through my motivational activity of introducing this build project. Part of this activity is asking the students how much experience they have building computers. Another question asked later is how many students want to build their own computer. From this activity, I would be able to observe the students' attitudes and excitement at having the opportunity to build a computer.

During instruction:
*Demonstration/instruction:* During the instruction process, I will be demonstrating how to connect various cables and components ultimately to build the computer. During the demonstration, volunteers will be asked to assist. Another source of data to analyze if the instruction is working or not will be the ability of the volunteers.

*Practice and feedback:* Following the demonstration, students will be split into groups of three to apply what they have just learned by practicing all of the demonstrated objectives. During this time, I (the instructor) will be going around to each group to offer feedback and suggestions if needed. Also, during this time I will be using a checklist to analyze if students are achieving the objectives or not. Collecting this data will help me determine, for future projects, if the instruction was good enough to help lead to an assessment.

Post-instruction:

*Assessment:* Students will then be able to build a computer on their own. During this assessment, I will have a checklist to use to determine if students are following the correct procedures to complete each of the five objectives. This checklist will provide essential data to determine the preparedness of the students for future projects. Once the students complete the steps, they will get instant feedback as to whether they built the computer correctly or not. If the computer turns on to the operating system, they built correctly. If the computer does not turn on, they have built incorrectly. This feedback will allow the students to go back and attempt to correct their mistakes. The feedback will be in written form through the use of the rubric/questions I have created in the "Tests" section. I would be able to use this data to find out which parts might need further instruction.

*Remedial:* Those students who were unable to have their computer boot to the operating system will be given the opportunity to correct their mistakes. This might require a complete rebuild. The students that did accomplish this task correctly will have the opportunity to help their fellow students fix their problems. I will be able to collect data through observation of the students correcting their mistakes and those students helping others. I will collect this data through a checklist and by having the students answer the following questions.
• What part of the build was incorrectly completed?
• What problems occurred that made you realize something was wrong?
• What steps did you take to troubleshoot the problem?
• How were you sure you corrected the problem?

*Attitude:* Following the instructional unit, I will pass out a questionnaire for the students to complete. This questionnaire will include questions such as:
• What did you like best about this lesson?
• What would you change about this lesson?
• Were there any parts that left you confused?
• What can you take away from this lesson that you will use out of school?
All of the data collected will be analyzed and will help me determine the changes that need to be made to this instructional unit to help the students learn more and to increase their enjoyment.

Revision:
Since I do not have access to the materials I would need, I was unable to implement my plan to collect the data. However, I have done the computer build project before and can look back at some of my previous experiences. I believe some parts of my assessment checklist will need to be revised to better suit the time allowed for the build project. I would also like to allow more time for practice and feedback.

**Figure 2.15** Computer build revisions plan

## Conclusion

Perhaps at this point you're feeling like this is a ridiculous length to go to for a single lesson. It definitely feels that way at first. But remember that when we started this journey together the idea wasn't to follow the model slavishly for each and every lesson, but to end up doing it a few times and carrying away some clear heuristics that can guide you into the future. To get started, you might select three or four really problematic lessons to use the process on and then see how going through this detailed process affects your other instructional designs in your classroom.

This chapter has presented the basics of the ID4T model. The steps may seem fairly time-consuming at this point; however, the reality of using basic ID principles in your instruction is that the heuristics and common errors can help to guide you in your everyday practices of ID in the classroom. In the chapters that follow we'll look at several special case issues such as the use of ID within a standards-based classroom, or when constructivism is the dominant theory of learning.

### What You Can Do Now (Chapter Summary)

At this point you will probably be able to:

- Outline the basic steps in the process of instructional design.
- Discuss how the steps in the ID process are related to one another.
- Distinguish a good learning goal from a poor one.
- Avoid typical errors in learning goal creation.
- Describe what CBC's role is in good learning objectives.
- Identify how you would go about gathering information on student characteristics and prerequisite skills.
- Distinguish between good and poor test items when given an objective.
- Select activities, texts, and media for a given learning goal and objectives.
- Lay out a plan for implementing your own instruction.
- Have some idea of what different steps look like in final projects.
- Create a plan for collecting data and revising instruction.

### Notes

1  Note that most examples will be presented alongside or just prior to feedback and improvement suggestions. Try to see if you can spot the weaknesses in the examples.

2 A rubric is a clear set of criteria that you would use to assess work, a sort of measuring stick that you can use to compare the work.

3 Note that group assessments can be part of an overall plan to test, but ultimately individual grades are required, so you may want a mix of assessment strategies that will evaluate a learner's ability in groups and individually.

4 Note that objectives for the purposes of instruction should not be written in the CBC format, but should instead be simplified, clear, and written at an appropriate reading level for the learners.

# 3

# How Does the ID4T Model Really Work in My Classroom?

## Chapter Questions

1. Which heuristic is going to be the easiest for you to integrate into your classroom?
2. Which heuristic is going to be the most difficult for you to integrate into your classroom?
3. Are the cases in this chapter true to what you think the use of ID in the classroom would look like?
4. How would you change the teachers' approaches in the cases?

## How Does This Model Really Work in My Classroom?

As I have already pointed out, this nine-step model probably feels nearly impossible to continuously and consistently apply to all instruction. After all, there are daily some six hours of instruction in most elementary classrooms. How could a kindergarten teacher apply these nine steps to every instructional moment? It would be an unwieldy process, bordering on cruelty, to teachers and students alike to expect anyone to engage in this model to the level that you'd have to the first time you use it for every moment of instruction. Rather, we need now to put together our list of heuristics and figure out what is the bottom line on the model and how it can best be used in the classroom on a daily and reasonable basis. This will help to review the main high points of the model and give you the tools to be able to learn to use this model as second nature. There may be some times when you really want to work on a particularly crucial or problematic lesson with the complete model from start to end, with careful and explicit attention to the nine steps, but by and large, I anticipate you'll find use of this model becomes much easier as you get more and more familiar with it. And to help you learn about the model and use it more quickly, review the following heuristics and put them together into a cohesive whole that will work for you in your own classroom. I believe this is the first step and the very best way to begin to understand how to really use this model in your classroom on a daily basis.

So, to review the heuristics, they are:

1. *Learning goals:* Ensure your learning goal is a clear, simple, single sentence that uses a measurable verb.
2. *Learning objectives:* Remember the lifeblood of your lesson is your CBC (condition, behavior, criterion) objective. Objectives should use *one* appropriate verb for a measurable behavior.
3. *Testing:* It is essential in good instruction that the testing and assessment is closely aligned with the behavior and conditions in the objectives.
4. *Prerequisites:* Make sure you have a clear sense of your learners; conduct a pre-test or survey to know for certain.
5. *Analysis of available texts:* Don't allow your texts to drive your instruction, use them as resources. Focus on the learning goal and select texts that meet your *most crucial learning needs.*
6. *Create and specify learning activities:* Select activities that best align with your instructional goal, objectives, and test items. Be careful not to use the same old activities that are most comfortable for you even if they do align with your lesson, and do not confuse activities and media.
7. *Selecting media:* Avoid selecting media too soon. Don't start your planning by saying, "This will be a PowerPoint lesson," or "This is going to be a video lesson." Select media that *support* your activities.
8. *Planning for implementation and trying it out:* Be prepared for failure and have a "Plan B" ready to go. Remain flexible. If you can try the instruction out with a small group first, give it a shot.
9. *Evaluating and revising the instruction:* Remember you can evaluate for improvement *and* decision making. Try to do both kinds of evaluation through test item analysis, surveys, interviews, and statistical analyses. Be cautious when relying on informal

data from the lesson and try to obtain formal data if you can. Revise, revise, revise!

This nine-step planning process will help you if you can keep these ideas tucked away in your head as you start to move into the planning processes. Often my students take 10–15 weeks to design a single hour of instruction to learn to use this model the first time around. But obviously no one would expect that to be the norm for most instructional moments. Rather we need to think about the ways that we can integrate this kind of thinking into everyday moments. Here are some examples of ways that might happen.

### Mrs. Debong's 1st Grade Classroom

Mrs. Debong arrived at her 1st grade classroom ready for the day. She had been particularly focusing on reading with her class over the first month of the school year. She was ready to introduce something new. She had already revisited beginning and ending and middle sounds and she felt pretty good that the learners were prepared to move on (*prerequisites*). Next, she wanted them to start really putting words together, to blend the sounds into words (*goal*). She knew there were several steps in learning to blend sounds including decoding the letters, stretching out the sounds, and distinguishing between sounds (*objectives*). She knew that the test items she'd prepare would have to directly assess the learners' abilities to decode, stretch, and distinguish sounds. She felt that an individual oral assessment was probably best (*testing*) and she created a little check sheet for each child to use when she or her para-professional checked their blending skills. She was already pretty clear on the basic content, having taught it for the past seven years, but she wondered if there might be something that could spice up the lessons and perhaps build a bit more relevance. She thought perhaps she'd seen something online, either a website or a handout, she couldn't quite recall. So she went and looked back at her bookmarked pages to see if she'd remembered to bookmark it and found several that related as well as some new ones (*review texts*). Based on these steps she began to determine how she might change the lessons surrounding learning to blend. She started

**Figure 3.1** ID4T works in the classroom!

to sketch out a few new activities (*activities*). And once she had planned out the activities, which included some discussion, demonstration, teacher modeling, and independent practice, she decided on several related media to support the lesson such as handouts/worksheets, website skills practice (*media*), and oral practice with the teacher, para-professional, and parent volunteers. She began to put the materials together and sketch out an approximate order for the various activities and lessons and how they would work together and take shape. Over the next two years she tried out the new lessons and made several changes to them until they met with her final approval (*implementation and revision*).

*Mr. Floyd's New Drums*

Mr. Floyd felt very lucky today indeed. The rotary club had donated a new drum set to one of his schools. Mr. Floyd was the music teacher in three different elementary schools and rotated from school to school delivering instrumental music lessons to 3rd, 4th, and 5th graders. To this point none of the schools had a really nice drum set, they mostly used practice pads and one school had a lower-end drum set without a lot of bells and whistles—literally. Now what was he going to do with it? Obviously, he knew that wasn't quite the right way to start things off, you can't choose the media before you figure out what your lesson goal is all about, so he thought more about why he had wanted to have the drum set in the first place. He had completed a grant application for the set and was lucky enough to have had the Rotary approve it. He pulled out the application to remind himself of his original goals. He had written that he had planned to have the drum set used for increased abilities in rhythm learning and for concerts. Hmmm, not all that helpful, but even though the words weren't there, he knew that there was more in his own mind when he'd written them and they did jog his memory a bit. So more specifically, he remembered that he had wanted to allow all the students to tap out different rhythms on different percussion instruments.

But he knew that a learning goal had to be more specific, so he decided to narrow it down to being able to read two measures of percussion music on a full drum set for any interested student (*goal*). He then broke the learning goal into a set of objectives, which he jotted down, focusing on just the behaviors to start (*objectives*). He jotted down, "Identify each part of drum set," "Correspond drum set part with musical notation," "Read two measures," but then he crossed out this last one, realizing that it was just a restatement of the goal statement, instead writing, "Distinguish between rhythms" (*objectives*). He knew he'd have to go into more detail about conditions and evaluations for these but decided to wait until the next day to tackle that. He turned off the light for the evening, tapping the high hat as he passed the new set. The next morning he spent another few minutes thinking through his drum set lesson. He knew that the primary condition for all of the objectives was to have a drum set at the ready;

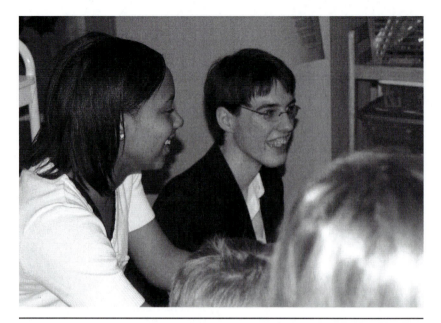

**Figure 3.2** Students benefit from ID4T in the classroom

however, he realized that he'd stated the goal was to read music, but he really wanted them to play the set, not just read it, so he re-adjusted his objectives and added a quick check sheet for himself to assess the learners' reaching the objectives (*objectives and testing*). He didn't feel all that comfortable about his learners' entry level skills because most of them hadn't had access to a real drum set, so he jotted down some questions he intended to ask them in class that day to see where they stood in their knowledge of the types of rhythms, names of instruments, and notation (*prerequisites*).

He checked the Internet to see if there were some good new sources to go with the new drum set. He found several, but with money tight and only one available as a free review copy, he ended up at the library and was able to find the other three sources to review that way (*texts*). Meanwhile he started thinking about the activities. Obviously not all of the students would be able to just sit down at the drum set and learn the notation there, so there had to be another way to use the set for demonstration. He puzzled over this for a while and ended up planning a demonstration and active questioning session (*activity*) using the drum set and a brief use of a website he found with a helpful link to the notation to the instrumentation (*media*). He knew that he had yet to review the texts in more detail and probably would want to work through the objectives with a bit more of a fine-tooth comb, but he decided to try it out with a small group of students he knew were particularly excited to get their hands on the drum set (*trial*). After the first run through, he saw that there were serious issues with the website's reliability and talked to the tech support folks to see if it was stable or if they had a better solution. The problem was internal to the school filters and was fixed for the next run through with a slightly larger group (*implementation, trials, revision*). He continued to revisit the drum lesson over the coming months to make sure that it was really doing what he wanted for new students as they became interested in the set.

In reality even this will seem, to many teachers reading this book, an impossible or unlikely way to approach preparing instruction. Shen, Poppink, Cui, & Fan (2007) wrote, "In the United States, planning and preparation are considered important, but lesson plans themselves seldom consist of more than a list of activities" (p. 248). What is common in lesson planning is a simple sit down over coffee very briefly to plan page numbers or new ideas during a planning session. But ID for teachers is a rather different approach. It may not take a lot more time as some of these examples illustrate—becoming more and more a part of your everyday work process. But it is very different from traditional planning.

Then what can we take from these examples? Primarily, while it may not *feel* like there's all that much of a difference in these cases from what would normally happen in teacher planning, there is in fact more alignment and intentionality with regard to what is happening in the learning than there might typically be. The question asked, for example, when testing is, "How can I align my tests with what I hope they'll be able to do at the end of the lesson?" not the more common, "What did I teach that I could put on the test?" And the activities are neither plucked from the air nor the old stand-bys used habitually. They are specifically focused and tailored for the instructional goal and objectives for that lesson. There is an acceptance that the whole thing isn't going to be done in a single moment or one planning session, but that the process will take time to refine, revise, and improve—that is the iterative nature of the planning process. There is even an acceptance that although any given teacher may not have had great success with a lesson today, there are many opportunities to review, reflect, revise, improve, and re-teach that material so that it becomes better and better as time goes by.

The primary notion in this chapter, then, is to put you on the front lines with the teachers who use this sort of instructional design process so that you can see how it can be used in your own practice. It is used not as a constrained set of rules, but rather as an opportunity to really align instruction in the way that research has told us is effective in reaching learners. Fill in your own blanks in one of the scenarios. Really try to take a moment to imagine yourself using this model for ID in your own classroom. Imagine yourself going through the steps for a bit of instruction that has perhaps become a little stale, or has never quite worked the way you think it should or could. This sort of imaging can help you actually *do* what you imagine you can do, it allows you a moment to go through the steps in your head and to see yourself being successful.

### What You Can Do Now (Chapter Summary)

At this point you will probably be able to:

- Describe and discuss ways that you can integrate the ID4T model into your own classroom right now.
- Create a case from your own classroom similar to those in this chapter to imagine a way that you could personally integrate the ID4T model into your own practice.

# 4

# How Can We Integrate Constructivist Notions into the ID4T Model?

## Chapter Questions

1. What is constructivism in the ID world?
2. Does this definition differ from what you thought constructivism was? If it does, in what ways?
3. What are the components of the constructivist classroom? Are there some you would add?
4. Do you think that the ID4T model will work in a constructivist classroom? Why/why not?

The ID4T model, like most of the traditional ID models, is really a behavioral model. What I mean by that is that you are looking specifically at the behavior that the learning creates and you're not all *that* interested in what goes on inside of the learner's head, only that they got it in a behaviorist sense, and that you reinforce it when they get it right. I discussed the major learning theories earlier in the book and I consider the ID4T model to be a mostly behaviorally oriented model. It is focused very closely on the behavior, on *what* the learner is doing. This model has most often led to a *direct* approach to instruction in which information is given directly to the learner and often the learner is then asked to do something with that information to show they are able to recall, apply, critique, or otherwise use the information they were given in the direct instruction.

The problem with this is that most of the recent research in the field of education has led us away from behaviorism (Ertmer & Newby, 2008). The majority of these folks have been saying for the previous 30 years or so that focusing exclusively on the behavior independent of what goes on inside the learner's own mind is really not productive. Behaviorism is thought of as the "black box" model of learning, because what is going on inside the learner's mind (the black box) isn't really important—the successful accomplishment of the learning goal, the performance, or behavior is what it's all about. In learning theories, cognitivism[1] came after behaviorism, which thought of the brain as a filing cabinet drawer and later a computer where information was filed away and the proper connections in the synapses would bring up the proper knowledge to accomplish a given task. The next evolution of learning theories was social constructivism and, in its most radical stance, constructivism purported that all knowledge is constructed (thus its name) inside the learner's head and then usually socially negotiated with those around them in a class.

This is a very different notion of learning and had very broad-ranging impacts on how we create learning environments and how we design classroom activities. This model is also seen as considerably more learner-centered because it realized that learning happens inside the learner's head and that the black box had to be opened up and understood as more than a mere filing cabinet. Now of course this is a very rudimentary and brief review of learning theories, and some might even say it's too simplistic, but I'd refer you to some of the great original learning theorists to really make sense of these three (Duffy & Jonassen, 1991; Jonassen, 1996; Merrill, 1991; Saettler, 1990; Skinner, 1948, 1971). Still the basic ideas of constructivism gave life to inquiry learning while the behaviorists might be said to have given life to the standards movement. The focus of standards or behaviorism tends to be the outcome, while the focus of constructivism is the process of learning.

Understanding what the components are of a constructivist learning environment or experience is the first place to begin our understanding of how the ID4T model could be adapted for use in a constructivist classroom. Before we start, however, it should be said that the model is most *easily* applied within a more traditional behavioral classroom. However, in my experience, constructivism and behaviorism are really more *beliefs* about how people learn than they are theories. Depending on what you believe about how learning happens and what the important outcomes are, you should try to pay either more or less attention to how to adapt this model for the constructivist classroom.

What Are the Components of a Constructivist Classroom?

Based on the beliefs that learners construct learning in their own heads and then socially negotiate it in a group, constructivist classrooms typically have the following components:

1. Authentic activities.
2. Social contexts.
3. Multiple perspectives.
4. Knowledge construction.
5. Metacognition (reflection on their own constructions).

Roblyer (1996) suggests, similarly, that constructivist classrooms have the following features:

1. Problem-based learning.
2. Group work (cooperative or collaborative).
3. Learning as exploration.
4. Authentic assessment (such as portfolios, products, performances).
5. Rich visual learning environments.

These are quite similar to the first list with a few differences, but the basics are there. This is a learning environment that is highly engaging for the learners, and not at all passive. Information is not passed on and tested; instead it is learned through experience and authentic activities. The environment includes good visuals, other people to learn from and with, and usually a variety of right answers or multiple perspectives on the problem rather than just one.

In addition to these classroom characteristics, there are several models out there that show a sort of sequence that constructivist classrooms should engage in. Perhaps among the simplest and easiest to use is Satchwell & Loepp's (2002) plans for middle-school engagement in math, science, and technology learning from a constructivist standpoint. They lay out a "learning cycle" in which the class follows an "Explore the idea, get the idea, apply the idea and expand the idea" sequence.

But then, given these characteristics and suggested sequence, how can our ID4T nine-step model work within constructivist classrooms? There are some conflicts that need to be worked through. For example, we want to set out an already established learning goal and a set of supporting objectives as part of the ID4T model. However, the constructivist classroom resists the notion of pre-established goals and objectives. Particularly for radical constructivists, it is more appropriate to allow the learner the ability to negotiate their goals with their teachers and classmates. But then doesn't that just leave us with no model at all? Hardly! We can (and ought to) carefully watch the unfolding of the constructivist classroom—even if it's a radically constructivist classroom—to see that there is alignment between the goals, however they are determined, and then tested. Scaffolding is a common concept in more recent conceptions of constructivist classrooms and the use of scaffolding can allow a bit more of a traditional tinge to the classroom experience by encouraging more directed scaffolding for learners. We ought to then ensure that authentic assessment really does measure what was intended in the learning. This is very similar to the expectation that testing would be aligned with our learning objectives as outlined in the original model.

To simplify, the constructivist-adjusted nine-step model looks a lot like this:

### Set Learning Goals

This may be done in collaboration with your learners, but it is important to ensure that you still have clearly stated goals that all agree upon. Approaching goals as a joint project along with your learners may feel a little uncontrolled at first, but ultimately this social negotiation process can be very powerful.

### Create Learning Objectives

For a constructivist classroom we should still have CBC as our lifeblood. While the objectives may be negotiated as the goals were, you'll still want to know precisely what the conditions, behavior, and criteria will be. The behavior is more likely in this case to be more open and at a higher level of learning (such as synthesize, evaluate, critique, negotiate, explore, analyze, and so forth).

### Create Authentic Testing

It is still essential to have well-aligned test items in the constructivist classroom, but your testing will be more authentic and will be likely to involve rubrics, performance checklists, and observations.

### Assess Prerequisites

This is a very important step in a constructivist classroom because it is even more based on the learners' own context and learning than in the more behavioral instruction. So make sure that you have a clear idea of where the learners are and that *they* have a clear idea of where they are as well.

### Analyze and Select Available Texts

Constructivist classrooms use texts much less often than do traditional classrooms. Someone once told me that if I see a lot of worksheets, it's probably not a constructivist classroom. The thing to understand here is not *whether* learning texts are used, but, rather, *how* they are used. If learners are expected to read, digest, and regurgitate a text in a test, this is definitely not true to the spirit of constructivist classrooms. If learning texts are used as support for the students as they pursue their own learning, then it is much more appropriate in the constructivist classroom. It is also important to remember that texts can be broadly defined, and authentic materials for problem-solving, such as those available in libraries and on the web, are rich sources of construction for all learners. Of course this step will have to wait until earlier steps, such as goals and objectives, are negotiated with the learners.

### Create and Specify Learning Activities

Once again we will want to see alignment here. In a constructivist classroom, authentic learning activities such as problem-based learning are going to be dominant. Thus, we need to ensure that these sorts of activities are well aligned with the earlier negotiated goals, objectives, and assessment plans.

Select Media

Constructivist classrooms tend toward technology solutions whenever possible. The reason for this is more historical than pedagogical, I believe—they both came into their own around the same time frame. Thus, often we'll see constructivist learning that is also technology-based. And while it is true that constructivist experiences do benefit from the availability of authentic materials for problem-based situations, for example, it is not essential that all constructivist environments engage high technology as the delivery media. While information resources have always been a part of constructivists' view of learning, interactive resources really fit well with what constructivists are trying to accomplish in the classroom. Once again, finding smart, efficient ways to use technology that clearly *align* with the needs of the instruction is the watchword.

### Plan for Implementing the Instruction, Trying It Out, Evaluating and Revising It

These last steps are almost always difficult in the constructivist classroom. Since it is unlikely that you'll really know for sure what the students will be looking for—what they will bring to the instruction, and how they will construct it—it becomes difficult to anticipate what will be tried out, what will be needed for effective implementation, how to evaluate, and whether to revise for next time. Rather, this becomes a series of self-reflections where the teacher can engage with the learners to help them the next time they wish to undertake a similar learning experience.

*A Case of ID for Teachers in a Constructivist Classroom*

Father Rinaldo taught at St. John's Catholic Preparatory School for more than 20 years and was pretty seasoned at it. He'd been well reared in the very traditional understandings of behavioristic learning models. However, one of his new student teachers, Joseph, had "preached" the gospel of constructivism to him until he was blue in the face and, in truth, Father had been pretty persuaded by it all. He checked out a few online and text resources about constructivism and thought that while it wouldn't work for some of his learners or some of the learning he intended for them to do, it could be compelling in his classes on marriage in particular. For some years he had been teaching the Healthy Relationships course which included units on romantic love, familial love, sibling relationships, relationships with parents and other elders, friendships, dealing with death, child rearing, and marriage. It was only a one-semester course, though it was required for all students. Father Rinaldo thought it was likely that much of the content in this particular course might lend itself well to the constructivist notions of learning. He was pretty sure that this wasn't really about memorizing the stages of death and grief—which had been a big part of his prior testing—but rather about helping his learners to construct their own understandings and socially negotiated meanings of issues such as marriage, death, and friendship. He decided to take the plunge (pardon the pun) with the marriage unit and create a constructivist-based lesson on the topic of gender roles in marriage. He knew that there was no single answer to what worked for so many different marriages, but rather that this topic might lend itself well to the social negotiation

Figure 4.1  ID4T allows for teachable moments

process and so he began by reviewing his old traditional lecture notes and materials to see where to start.

Father Rinaldo found his old notes and the learning goal and objectives scribbled haphazardly along the top margin. He recalled the idea of goals/objectives sort of being an add-on at the time and smiled to himself. So many waves of change, hard to know what may come next, he reflected. He jotted down the goal and objectives and thought about how best to present them to the learners to get their input. He wasn't really used to breaking away from the traditional lecture mode that he used for most of the course and it took a bit of courage to present negotiable goals and objectives. He presented them about one week prior to the unit start in order to give himself a little time to do some planning. The learners hadn't changed his goals and objectives very much, and he worried that they might have wanted to, but, like him, they were caught a little off guard by being able to negotiate the nature of the content. Perhaps things would unfold a bit more freely as they delved into the unit. They had determined that the goal was to "develop a deep understanding of gender roles in marriages" and the learners *had* indicated that there were some different types of marriages, as had been discussed earlier in the course, and that roles were definitely going to be related to marital type. He was encouraged by this connection. Objectives included things like defining several types of gender roles, describing the type of marital roles the learners hoped to have in their own marriages, discussing what these roles might mean for daily tasks and divisions of labor. At the point the objectives were presented to the learners they were more like topics to be covered rather than more formal learning objectives. He put the objectives into CBC format and posted them so that the learners would be clear about how they'd be evaluated and under what conditions he expected that the learning would be demonstrated (*goals and objectives*). But he felt that he'd taken a step back after he posted the objectives on the first day of the unit because the learners seemed to be annoyed that the traditional form of goal/objectives had been posted. He always felt that it was only fair to the learners to know what was expected of them, but he worried that he'd done the wrong thing here to have a clearly stated goal and objectives. All he could do was go forward now and try to encourage as much constructivist learning as possible.

During the planning period, Father Rinaldo started by thinking through how he'd know if his learners had really learned what he hoped they would. He knew that within a constructivist classroom it wasn't about some multiple-choice test, and he was glad to break away from that, particularly in this context. He thought he might do some assessments of roleplays where he could observe some of their negotiations about daily tasks. He also planned to do some evaluations of communication patterns in different role types and he created rubrics and checklists for both of these, which were aligned to measure his objectives (*tests*). While Father Rinaldo felt pretty clear about where his learners were in their learning about marriages and relationships, having followed their development for the past six weeks already, he felt that it was worthwhile in a constructivist environment to make sure he knew more about where they were with gender roles and prerequisites to constructing their learning about gender roles. He also felt it was pretty important to make sure that his students knew where they were in their own learning since they were negotiating it and learning it as a *group*. So he did a self-check form to be distributed before the start of the session (*prerequisites*). He then turned his attention back to the objectives and checked his usual textbook. He found that it really wasn't addressing the kinds of questions that his learners had highlighted as being interesting to them, and decided instead on the *Living together in marriage* text, which is used in Pre-Cana² classes. He worried that it might be too adult but as he reviewed it, it became clearer that there was good alignment and the reading level was that of about 8th grade, so he decided to use that one. He would make copies of the relevant section as the students didn't really need to have the entire text (*text selection*).

Next, Father Rinaldo looked at activities and media in combination. He decided that roleplays would be a really strong activity to illustrate the points that the learners were trying to better understand. He also felt open discussions and a debate were in order. He fleshed out these ideas more fully to ensure good alignment and planning and then turned to the media. In really looking at his activities and the types of things they were going to do, he determined that no advanced media/technology was really needed. He felt that he *could* use the SMART board or a simulation, and he found an interesting video series, but none of them would really work well with what had been negotiated already with the learners (*activities and media*). Father Rinaldo reflected that this made things a bit easier in terms of technological implementation. At least he wouldn't have to contact Brother Paul for anticipated help with the technology. But he did still need to pay very close attention to the parental communications. That was always the case, but in a constructivist environment where things were a little more free-wheeling and more learner-centered, he realized that it could be a real issue for parent communication and he planned carefully for an introduction letter to the unit and then a couple of intermittent emails. He drafted the first parts of the emails so that he'd have them prepared and be reminded to send them, but of course he wasn't able to really flesh out the details until the sessions ran and he had something important to share with the parents (*implementation*). He felt a little uneasy but well prepared as he went into the first class session. After the sessions were completed he did a brief survey with the students and a careful item analysis on their tests for the unit to determine if this gender roles section had fared well. He knew he couldn't do much about pre-planning for the next time because the energy came as a result of the learners' input and that would be unique to each group; nevertheless, he thought it important to reflect and he did come up with a short list of things he might like to do differently next time (*evaluation*).

**What You Can Do Now (Chapter Summary)**

At this point you will probably be able to:

- Describe what constructivism is and its relationship to your own practice and your own classroom.
- List the critical components of the constructivist classroom.
- Explain the ways in which the ID4T model can work with the constructivist classroom.
- Describe a lesson you use that is constructivist in nature and how it might work with the ID4T model.

## Notes

1 Constructivism does pre-date cognitivism when traced to Piaget in the 1930s, though social constructivism is more recent and more associated with the term.
2 This is a Roman Catholic marriage preparation program with well-researched documents which cover what the Catholic Church finds to be the most common issues in marriage—communication, money, and sex.

# 5

# How Can We Integrate User-Design into the ID4T Model?

**Chapter Questions**

1. What is user-design in the classroom?
2. How do you think user-design works with ID in your own words?
3. What are the components of the user-design classroom? Are there some you would add/change?
4. Do you think that the ID4T model will work in a user-design classroom? Why/why not?
5. How do you think you would approach user-design ID in your classroom?

User-design (UD) is another relatively new student-centered model for creating good learning environments. As with constructivism, user-design empowers learners to create their own learning, but user-design is less well known and has fewer significant research studies to back it up. Nevertheless, user-design is one of the most powerful new tools coming into the classroom today for the creation of truly student-centered learning (Carr-Chellman, 2006).

User-design has primarily been applied to the systemic change of whole-school systems, typically at the district level. In this, user-design has been seen as a way to engage a wide variety of users of a school in the creation or re-creation of educational systems from buildings to curricula.

Most simply defined, user-design classrooms are ones in which the learners not only select their own learning goals, as in the constructivist classroom, but also engage in the creation of those learning environments which will then support their goals. The users are designing, not just informing, the ultimate design.

User-design in the classroom implies empowering learners in significant ways. This is also seemingly at odds with traditional goal-setting by the teacher and tendency toward expertism within traditional ID models. This chapter addresses ways in which UD can be a part of ID4T in the classroom by allowing the learners to select the goals and objectives where possible and then creating effective high-quality instruction by thinking about these basic ID principles with the learners themselves.

**What Are the Components of a
User-Design Classroom?**

Based on the beliefs that learners are the users and therefore the best instructional designers, user-design classrooms have the following components:

1. Goals are set by learners.
2. Learners create experiences to support goals.
3. Teachers support the design process and are experts in design.
4. Classrooms are resource rich and experiences outside the classroom are common/expected.
5. Design is taught explicitly.
6. Collaboration is common and expected.
7. Community resources are brought into the classroom.
8. Assessment and accountability are based on learner accomplishment and self-evaluation/reflection.

Just like constructivist classrooms, user-design classrooms are the farthest thing from a passive learning experience. Once again, learning is experienced through authentic activities, but these are activities that the learners themselves have created—ones which they believe will bring them closer to achieving their own learning goals. This is, perhaps, the most learner-centered model presented in this book, and is highly experimental. There are several schools that are close to user-design such as a variety of "democratic" schools in which rules are set collaboratively. However, true user-design schools engage in the process of design in much more significant ways than most democratic schools. So, if it's rather rare and experimental, why even consider it in this book?

User-design has perhaps the largest potential to unlock exciting new paradigms of learning and is becoming more interesting to many in the educational field. Reviewing it here and thinking through how ID4T could be successfully worked into a UD classroom is worthwhile.

As already suggested, user-design shares a good deal with its cousin the constructivist classroom. Both are student-led and focus on meaningful learning that is highly relevant to the learner (since it often, though not always, is student choosing which directs their learning in both cases). Both constructivist and user-design classrooms expect teachers to be primarily mentors or facilitators. However, the constructivist classroom usually does acknowledge the teacher as an expert in knowledge to be shared with the learner even if it is from within a constructivist experience of the information, while the user-design teacher is more of an expert in design and less of an expert in any given topic(s). Both are empowering models of learning in which control is significantly shared. Both of these models are time consuming, and user-design is largely untested. Sometimes in order to create any level of efficiency in the classroom, consensus has to be sought and this can undermine the need for individual learners to reach their own goals. This is more frequent and common in the constructivist classroom currently than in the user-design classroom. Both of these models go against the traditional classroom systems that are set up for more direct instruction models.

User-design schools are risky because they allow the learner so much freedom; however, for the same reason they can be incredibly powerful. The ID process in user-design classrooms is less efficient because designing and learning are happening at the same moment they are co-evolving. In order to make our basic nine-step ID model work in a user-design setting, we'll have to again revisit the process in significant ways. While much of the basic framework remains, the attention to design process is heightened in this environment.

### Set Learning Goals

This will always be done in collaboration with your learners. Clarity is still very important, and helping the learners to see the difference between clear and "muddy" goals or even compound goals is critical.

Teaching the learner about appropriate verbs and scope for goals for a given time period is also critical. Goals need not necessarily be negotiated with whole groups. Individual goals are acceptable and group goals are also encouraged; helping learners to see the differences, and to meet their own goals within a group goal are all part of the design of instruction in a user-design ID model for classrooms. Thus we see the need for not only the learning of the content itself that is being examined, but also the need to learn about the process of design as well. Initially this can create a feeling that the learning is far less efficient but in reality we are also fulfilling a need for the learner to learn how to design. Another advantage of this approach is that the learners develop executive functions and self-regulation.

### Create Learning Objectives

In a user-design classroom we have to carefully explain why conditions, behaviors, and criteria are important aspects of a negotiated set of learning objectives. Students are creating their own objectives, not just goals, so they must understand what can make a great learning objective that will work for them and motivate them. The learner must specify precisely what the conditions, behaviors, and criteria will be. Behaviors may range from low through high levels of learning taxonomies (recall, analyze, synthesize, demonstrate, etc.) depending on what the learner is aiming for.

### Create Authentic Testing

This is one of the most difficult tasks in a user-design classroom because learners have to create their own tests. Most learners will be thrilled with this idea at first, until it becomes clearer that creating a good test that is well aligned is really tough to do and needs a good deal of guidance and scaffolding. First this all feels pretty weird—aren't we giving away the answers? Well yes, in a way we are, but they are the answers that the learner has to find for themselves, so even at a recall level, memorization is a task the learner must master. It remains essential that all test items are properly aligned with the goals and objectives, and teaching the learners what that means and why that's important is a vital step in this part of the process in a user-design classroom. It is quite likely that authentic assessments in this case will involve significant interactions with people and contexts outside the classroom.

### Assess and Fill Prerequisites

The nice thing about user-design is that prerequisite knowledge, once that concept is clear to learners, is actually innate and does not require a great deal of explication. The learner simply needs to list his or her preparations and identify any gaps. Group learning can require more discussion of prerequisite learning. Once again, ensuring that the learners understand what a prerequisite is and what role it plays in the creation of their own learning is the primary focus of this step. Because the learner is able to identify their own prerequisites they are also encouraged at this moment to fill those prerequisite gaps now rather than waiting for the "end" of the design process—rather *design and learning happen concurrently.*

### Analyze Available Texts

This actually becomes a rather difficult step in the user-design classroom. Most students are disinterested in analyzing books when it is first mentioned, and creating their own learning is now becoming a bit tedious. Remember, the process takes a lot longer in user-design classrooms, particularly the first few times through. This step can be very exciting when the learners realize that the world is their text and that they can consider many different resources online and offline to inform their learning. As the learners are selecting their texts, they are also using their texts to inform the next step in the process activities design. The learners should take the texts and resources and use them, learning from them as they create their activities.

### Create and Specify Learning Activities and Media, Evaluate and Revise the Design

Learning activities creation in the user-design classroom is the most wonderful part of the process. The same sort of energy that teachers feel when they create fun learning experiences is unleashed for learners, but not only are they creating the learning activities, they're *doing* them at the same time. They are able to rapidly move through these phases and activities as they learn which activities work effectively and which are less than optimal. Thus the activities step begins to engage the entire rest of the process as learners must select appropriate learning media, try things out, evaluate those activities, and revise them in order to effectively reach their own goals. It is important throughout this complex interplay of several steps that the learners are maintaining good design, and the teacher should help to ensure this is happening. Ongoing negotiation among team members in group-learning environments will make this a complicated dance of design, creation, trying out, evaluating, and keeping/rejecting ideas and experiences. It is during this stage that the learners are going out into the community to find their learning environments through internships, or meetings, attendance at political rallies, and the like. Learners are most fully engaged in these last few steps, but the teacher must ensure that good design rules continue to be followed. It is important that the teacher offers guidance as to the extent of alignment among activities and goals and other parts of the process. The learners may need some scaffolding and guidance during this stage but they do not need to have someone *tell* them the answers. UD is definitely a process of design and discovery in powerful partnership.

*A Case of ID for Teachers in a*
*User-Design Classroom*

Gifted education had challenged Mr. Broadsom for years. The notion of *who* was gifted or G & T—gifted and talented as they called it— was mysterious. The tests weren't reliable and the distinctions ended up being as much about school behavior and success as they were about real intelligence. He had a rather unusual G & T class that he thought might be a good candidate for a user-design approach, which he'd heard about at a conference a year or so earlier. The notion of the power that *might* be unleashed in a UD classroom was appealing, but it also sounded complex and cumbersome. Mr. Broadsom was sure that he couldn't use UD in his other non-gifted classes because he had serious state standards pressures there, but maybe the G & T class offered an opportunity.

The course was on 11th grade computer programming in the high school. Mr. Broadsom had taught this course many times, and was always struck by the combination of shop-like feel mixed with the gifted learners. It was a really strange place at times, but one that he thought offered a significant opportunity to try out some user-design ideas. He thought UD sounded like a really wonderful way to get yourself into some pretty interesting predicaments. After all, it was one thing to *consider* the learner in your own design, but another to *empower* them to create it themselves. Well, he figured if anyone could, maybe his gifted kids could, but then again they were kind of locked into the standard way that schools operate, that's part of why they ended up in G & T classes. So he was quite unsure of what to expect.

He started by discussing with the class his ideas for looking at user-design in their unit on designing computer games.[1] The group clarified their learning goals. Since this was an empowerment exercise it was vitally important that the learners really felt that anything, or almost anything, was allowed. They suggested some gaming ideas that were pretty gory, but Mr. Broadsom allowed all discussions at this point—he recognized it as brainstorming as well as testing to see if they really could do whatever they wanted as long as they were actually learning about game design. It appeared that they could. In the end, the students needed a little help with making clear goals, but the *content* of the goals wasn't influenced by Mr. Broadsom at all and they ended up with, "The learners will create a working game following basic gaming conventions" (*goal*). The objectives seemed to be a bit easier for the class to create. In fact, they kept wanting to write objectives during the goal portion; getting more specific was easier than the global task for some reason. They ended up with several objectives and needed some direction from Mr. Broadsom about how to ensure they were measurable or how to include appropriate conditions and why that was important. The nice thing was that it all made easy sense to them as far as the CBC structure. They included objectives on the length of the game, the minimal number of rules, several other gaming conventions, and then included an objective on reflecting on the game design process itself. Mr. Broadsom felt things were off to a great start.

The students were very energized by being able to really build whatever they wanted. Where gaming was concerned, they had been censored most of their educational lives, and the freedom was intoxicating—truth be told it might have been a little scary for some of them though. They decided that testing wasn't really appropriate in the traditional sense, but the class created a nice check sheet to ensure that all games had the basic conventions that they thought were important enough to include in their goals and objectives (*test*). Likewise, a check sheet was created to ensure that everyone in the class had the necessary tools to do the job of creating games and all learners were encouraged to do some serious self-reflection as they'd be working in teams for the most part and didn't want to let their colleagues down (*prerequisites*). Mr. Broadsom worried that the class would get bogged down in the next few steps because they'd be frustrated by all the planning being pushed onto the students rather than having it all laid out for them, but to his surprise the learners were really excited about looking at texts and online resources for game design as well as thinking through what kinds of activities would be best for their lesson (*texts and activities*).

For the most part, the students weren't all that creative, particularly where activities were concerned. They were willing to really branch out where texts were concerned, and were interested in critically analyzing what texts might be useful, but their activities were really focused on lots of time coding and designing and they followed a fairly traditional game design trajectory. Naturally the media they selected were computers based primarily on their goals to create computer games so they didn't spend much time specifying the media, though Mr. Broadsom did encourage them to think carefully about the tools they used to create the games, so there was some consideration given to media (*media*). As they went along, they self-evaluated to see what was working and what wasn't. They looked at their team processes, the tools they used, the texts that informed them, the various models of games that they considered and the activities they engaged in daily for more than three weeks as they built their own games. They were able to tell a great deal to Mr. Broadsom as they

**Figure 5.1** ID4T works with active learning

wrapped up the unit and described what worked and what didn't work and what they would do differently next time (*implementation and evaluation*). They absolutely felt that the user-design process was great and wanted to repeat it again later in the year. Mr. Broadsom had feared that the students would be limited by their narrow definitions of success in the classroom, and that they would resist the planning process, but instead they had really enjoyed the process and a lot of energy was released as a result of the empowerment.

**What You Can Do Now (Chapter Summary)**

At this point you will probably be able to:

- Describe what user-design is and its relationship to your own practice and your own classroom.
- List the critical components of the user-design classroom.
- Explain the ways in which the ID4T model can work with the user-design classroom.

• Describe a lesson you use that is user-design in nature and how you might work with the ID4T model.

## Note

1  I appreciate Luis Almeida's contributions here, as his dissertation was on this topic.

# 6

# How Can We Integrate Inquiry Learning into the ID4T Model?

**Chapter Questions**

1. What is inquiry learning?
2. Does this definition differ from what you thought inquiry learning was? If it does, in what ways?
3. How does inquiry learning work with ID4T in your own words/ ideas?
4. What are the components of the inquiry classroom? Are there some you would add?
5. Do you think that the ID model will work in an inquiry classroom? Why/why not?
6. How do you think you would approach inquiry learning ID in your classroom?

Inquiry learning is perhaps among the most popular recent trends in learning environment design and curricular change. Inquiry learning has been primarily aimed at science education (rather than language or mathematics) but the basic premises could actually be applied to any learning content. The basic idea of inquiry learning is that we should start with learners' questions—their inquiries—and that should be the foundation of our teaching. As with user-design and constructivist classrooms, inquiry-based classrooms stray far from the more traditional direct instruction-based philosophies of a "sage on the stage" and focus instead on the teacher as a "guide on the side." The teacher's role is more to mentor and facilitate than to instruct students. However, the teacher in the inquiry-based classroom is facilitating the process of knowledge discovery. This is in contrast to the user-design model in which the teacher facilitates the process of *design*. All three of these models are considered learner centered and tend to agree with most recent theories of learning.

What Are the Components of an
Inquiry Classroom?

Inquiry classrooms are usually places of great activity, where learners are pursuing their questions with delight and excitement. Because inquiry classrooms start with the learners' questions, they are rarely places of tedium—at least for the learners. Typically, inquiry classrooms:

- Are driven by student questions.
- Use "open learning" as a cornerstone (in which students do not have pre-specified targets or goals to accomplish).
- Are discovery oriented.
- Are heavily group-oriented.
- Are driven by a stimulus—typically a teacher-posed question, or (preferably) a student-posed question in the form of a big or guiding question.
- Are flexible, can engage projects that are narrow or broad, creative, laboratory oriented, experimental, etc.
- Work well in interdisciplinary units (though that hasn't been the dominant model for inquiry-based classrooms to this point).

Inquiry classrooms require a great deal of careful planning and organization. Curry, Cohen, & Lightbody (2006) suggest that these forms, along with technology, create a very learner-centered environment, much like user-design or constructivist classrooms. And these environments must attend to diverse student populations: "Science curricula featuring inquiry must be informed by tools, strategies, and methods designed to meet the needs and preferences of diverse learners" (p. 37).

Marshall, Horton, & White (2009) have identified a set of levels associated with the inquiry process in classrooms: pre-inquiry (level 1), developing inquiry (level 2), proficient inquiry (level 3), and exemplary inquiry (level 4). Likewise, Krajcik, McNeill, & Reiser (2007) argue that science should be learned by doing science rather than being told about science:

> Developing learning performances also supports project-based pedagogy, by embedding the commitment to apply science to problems directly into the articulation of learning goals. Furthermore, the learning performances allow us to look at the same content across different inquiry practices

and the same inquiry practices across different content to create a more complete picture of a student's understanding. (p. 24)

Unlike constructivism and user-design, inquiry learning lends itself more readily to some kinds of learning over other kinds of learning. That is, science learning has been the focus of most inquiry-based learning to date; however, anywhere that a child has a question or inquiry can easily be turned into an opportunity to use inquiry learning. This means that, in some cases, inquiry learning is not the best choice, and determining first if the type of learning that is being addressed is best served by an inquiry approach may be the first pre-step before approaching our nine-step ID4T model. The nine steps are:

## Determine the Appropriateness of the Inquiry Model

In this step it will be important for the teacher to determine the extent to which the specific learning is open to inquiry. Is the learning best framed by a question? Will the question interest learners? The power of inquiry learning is the increased motivation as a result of the focus on learner questions and discovery. If this is not the case, it is perhaps best to turn to one of the other learning approaches.

## Set Learning Goals

Goals are set alongside learners often by a stimulus question on the part of the teacher or a student or a group of students. If any guidance is offered in inquiry learning from the teacher it is likely to be in the form of a question not a statement. The goal of the learning will typically be to answer the question, be it from a teacher or learner. The goal is a cooperative one, and thus goal negotiation will be an important part of a clearly worded goal that is understood and accepted by all in the classroom.

## Create Learning Objectives

For an inquiry classroom we should hold on to the usefulness of CBC. The objectives and goals are both negotiated in the inquiry classroom as they were in the user-design and constructivist classrooms. Nevertheless it is important, particularly in this group negotiation situation, to know precisely what the conditions, behaviors, and criteria will be. As in the constructivist classroom, the behavior is likely to be more open and at a higher level of learning (such as synthesize, evaluate, critique, negotiate, explore, analyze, and so forth).

### Create Authentic Testing

It is still essential to have well-aligned test items in the inquiry classroom. Since the inquiry classroom has mostly focused on scientific learning, it is likely that the testing will align with scientific instruction and standards. The authenticity of these tests will be important in that scientific learning is very often grounded in discovery and reporting, as well as making new connections and synthesizing findings. Thus, in this case, authentic testing should also take good science teaching practices into account.

### Assess Student Characteristics and Entry Level Behaviors

Scientific learning, and inquiry learning more generally, is clearly laid on the foundations of prior learning. Perhaps more so than in other kinds of learning, understanding the prerequisites of a given goal as well as the understandings and prior knowledge of your learners will be very important in the inquiry classroom. Surveys and pre-tests are highly recommended in this case. While it can be much more optional in other situations and it is time consuming, it is also important to ensure in inquiry (as in math learning) that the basic building blocks are well established first.

### Analyze the Available Texts

Texts in the inquiry classroom are important foundations for question formation and progress. Because inquiry learning is based on the kinds of questions that learners ask, forming those questions from within a given text will help to marry the inquiry classroom with the standards movement as discussed next. Text selection again should be made without too many constraints. Avoid using the dry old science textbook and try to find new resources that may be more interdisciplinary and current, which can stimulate questions on the part of students. Introducing novelty in the text can help to stimulate questions as well.

## Create and Specify Learning Activities

As with text selection, novelty and motivation are important in forming a good inquiry classroom environment. Surprising and unexpected results can often stimulate excellent question formation on the part of the learner. Activities should try to allow for open-ended learning with a discovery bent. Recall Marshall, Horton, & White's (2009) suggestions in terms of phases of inquiry, as this can help you order the activities and give a sense of sequence to the lessons. Here we hope to see activities that encourage pre-inquiry, developing inquiry, proficient inquiry, and exemplary inquiry.

## Select Media

Without a doubt, inquiry classrooms are very likely to involve or include technology sources. But sometimes it is best to consider low-tech solutions to inquiry-based learning environments. Once again, wisdom is found in caution here. Using the proper tool for the situation is key and using a more expensive or "glitzy" solution isn't appropriate if it doesn't advance the needs of the learners as they embark on their inquiry learning goal. Considering new media alongside innovative texts and novel activities will probably produce a very strong lesson, but may be overwhelming in the "newness" of everything for the learner. So keeping some things that are familiar and comfortable may make sense as well. The primary goal is alignment among the goals/objectives/tests/activities and then subsequent media and text decisions.

## Plan for Implementing the Instruction, Trying It Out, Evaluating and Revising It

Naturally, inquiry learning will give many opportunities for iterations in the classroom. If an inquiry lesson doesn't work the first time, and the goal is not reached, then consider alterations to the plan, inclusion of different materials or media, or changes in the activities. Since most inquiry learning is done in groups, it is worth going back through the process until the learning has been accomplished for the entire group. Thus "trying it out" usually will not happen in small groups first, but rather as a large group. In that case, alterations will take place during the lesson and after each lesson in the sequence of lessons, such that subsequent lessons can also be improved and brought into alignment with the direction of the inquiry learning experience.

*A Case of ID for Teachers in an Inquiry Classroom*

Mr. Carson adored science and loved the experience of awakening young minds to the real joys of science. As a 2nd grade teacher it had always been his favorite subject to teach his little ones. He loved to see the light bulbs go on and the excitement the children had over each new discovery, as if new worlds were opening to them. Mr. Carson had read a book on inquiry learning over the summer and decided that he wanted to try an inquiry lesson or unit. He knew that the questions had to come from the students so, after he had read the book, he had to really check his own enthusiasm and wait for the kids to come in with an exciting question.

It happened on the first crisp day of fall. One of the children, Sonya, brought in a caterpillar, a "fuzzy wuzzy" as the kids called it. Mr. Carson enjoyed the excitement over the caterpillar that was unleashed when Sonya shared it with the class in its little glass jar with milkweed leaves for food and a stick to climb. The kids ooed and aaahhed over it for some time. Finally, one of them started, "Why does it have all that fuzz anyway?" Another answered, "So it can become a butterfly, silly." "Are you sure, I mean what does that fuzz have to do with it becoming a butterfly? How does it become a butterfly?" "Yeah how does that happen?" More children chimed in, "Oh you know they get into the cocoon and when they come out they're butterflies, we learned about that in kindergarten." "*I* learned about that in preschool." "Well anyway, that's why." It seemed the matter was settled completely. But Mr. Carson knew he could use this as a first step in an inquiry lesson or unit. The unit on the lifecycle of the butterfly wasn't actually scheduled until later in the year, but really the time was now to jump on this, and so he did.

"Do you all really know how a butterfly comes to be?" The children looked wide-eyed, "Not really, it—" "No." "It just happens." "My mom told me it was magic fairies." "That's not true!" "Yes it is, my mom told me." "Would you like to learn more about that?" asked Mr. Carson. The explosion of enthusiasm was heard all the way across the hall and down to the principal's office. The children most definitely did want to know how a butterfly comes to be from a caterpillar (*goal*). "All right then, since sharing is over, let's start by getting to our desks and we can start to write down our questions about caterpillars and butterflies." It took some time for the questions to be written, but there was a remarkable amount of quiet and concentration. Occasionally someone would raise their hand to ask how to spell a word or how to express something they were confused by. Mr. Carson was excited too, it seemed that taking the learners' questions seriously was pretty powerful.

Mr. Carson looked at all the pieces of paper with all the kids' questions. Jaimie had even asked whether moms can tell lies and why they'd do that. Clearly there wasn't quite as much focus as was going to be needed to put together a good unit on the lifecycle of the butterfly. So Mr. Carson looked them over and came up with a couple of options that he presented to the class the next day. He knew that negotiating the goals and objectives would have to be done as a whole group and that inquiry learning was highly dependent on learner empowerment so he wanted to try to give the students a lot of decision making in the process. They all agreed on the learning goal and objectives and even some sub-objectives. They weren't called that, of course, but instead were "Our question" and "How we'll answer our question: steps" which seemed to work fine for the learners' understanding of what was expected in the coming weeks. Mr. Carson took the "How we'll answer our question: steps" and turned them into more formal objectives that included CBC components only for himself, and made sure that the critical aspects of evaluation or conditions were communicated at the proper times to the class (*objectives*). Mr. Carson knew that the children had learned about butterflies several times before, it was included in the kindergarten curriculum briefly and a little more in depth in 1st grade, and some of them apparently even had some experience of it in pre-school, though he doubted much of that would come to play in his 2nd-grade classroom (*prerequisites*). He had a pretty clear idea of what was already learned, but he did talk with the kids a bit more about it to make sure. Knowing that science is always about building blocks of learning from one level to the next, he wanted to be sure of where he was with his learners. He also created assessments for himself that were really checklists that would allow him to keep track of the progress of each student through interviews or discussions (*tests*). Mr. Carson already had all of his materials on the lifecycle of the butterfly, but he did review them carefully to make sure that they really aligned with the questions that the learners were asking. He found that one set of materials wasn't very useful for the kinds of things that the learners wanted to know and so he set that aside. He thought if he used it later in the year that would be fine, but it might also just be a resource he'd have to sacrifice this time around (*review texts*).

Mr. Carson was enchanted by the excitement that the learners were showing, but he also was concerned about too much free and open learning. He wanted to have some structure around the class activities. He decided to use the pre-inquiry, developing inquiry, proficient inquiry, and exemplary inquiry phases and started creating a variety of activities that were novel and directed right at the learners' questions. He knew he'd have to remain flexible and ditch some of them if they weren't working, but he decided to at least have something well planned for the lessons . . . he just wasn't comfortable with too loose a structure (*activities*). He also knew of several good resources, movies, internet sites, and a couple of simulations that allowed the learners to play with things like the amount of food, temperature, etc., to see what happens to the development of the butterfly given different variables. He wasn't entirely sure that they'd fit in, but he reviewed and prepped them in case he could use them (*media*). He needed to be sure that the activities and the media really followed the kids and where they wanted to go with the inquiry rather than fitting into his comfort zone of having something scheduled and planned for every minute of the school day. He checked in with the administration to make sure that a change in schedule was all right and wouldn't upset the apple cart too

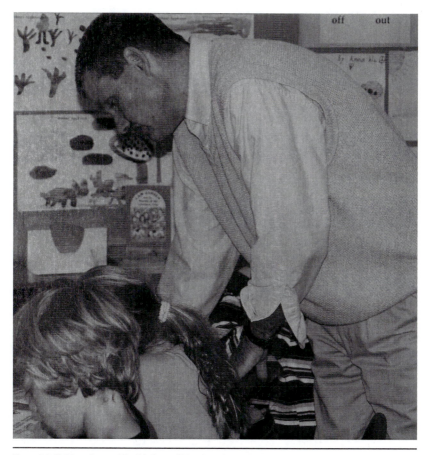

**Figure 6.1** ID4T can be used flexibly for traditional or alternative learning modes

much in terms of alignment with other classrooms. He also checked in with the technical support person, Ed, to make sure that the various things needed for the technology use were going to be supported, available, and working when he needed them (*implementation*). Finally, as the unit unfolded, Mr. Carson found himself revising some of his materials and revising some of the procedures to make sure that everyone could learn the important phases of the butterfly lifecycle that would be important later and that would/could really answer the questions that the learners had (*evaluation and revision*). It was an amazing experience and he felt that the learning had, surprisingly, not become stale. He had expected that once the novelty of inquiry learning had worn off, the learners would lose their interest and it would be back to the same old, same old. He was wrong, in fact. Near the end of the unit, students started asking if they could ask another question and another … They had loved the experience of having some power over their own learning and answering their own questions.

**What You Can Do Now (Chapter Summary)**

At this point you will probably be able to:

- Describe what inquiry learning is and its relationship to your own practice and your own classroom.
- List the critical components of the inquiry classroom.
- Explain the ways in which the ID4T model can work with the inquiry classroom.
- Describe a lesson you use that is inquiry learning in nature and how you might work with the ID4T model.

# 7

# HOW CAN WE INTEGRATE THE STANDARDS-BASED CURRICULUM INTO THE ID4T MODEL?

## Chapter Questions

1. What are standards and why do you think we have them?
2. How is the standards movement different from constructivism, user-design, and inquiry learning?
3. Does this definition and motivation for using standards differ from what you thought standards were? If it does, in what ways?
4. What are the components of the standards-based classroom? Are there some you would add?
5. Do you think that the ID model will work in a standards-based classroom? Why/why not?
6. How do you think you would approach standards-based ID4T in your classroom?

And now for something completely different! Running almost counter to all of the prior alternatives to the traditional ID4T model that we have discussed (constructivist classrooms, user-design, and inquiry learning) thus far, is the standards movement. This was highlighted most recently with the movement toward the Common Core or what is officially known as the Common Core State Standards (CCSS). Because of the politically charged nature of standards, we'll take up a brief discussion of the movement as a whole here. The standards movement most succinctly defined is primarily a political effort to ensure accountability in the classroom by specifying very clear learning goals and outcomes. Formalized by the Bush administration's No Child Left Behind (NCLB) legislation, standards-based classrooms live with mandated standards that each child must meet in order to be considered on grade level. However, the standards movement started long before NCLB. Buttram & Waters (1997) write,

> With the publication of the *Nation at risk* report, elected officials and policymakers began demanding that educators be held accountable for results. This switch in emphasis (from input to results) set the stage for the delineation of standards, or what students should know and be able to do . . . Elected officials and policy makers see standards-based education as a powerful tool for improving the outcomes of public education for students. (p. 2)

Buttram & Waters point to the positive outcomes of communities determining what standards would be in their schools, or disciplines negotiating what would be required of learners at different levels. "This process of identifying and setting standards helps clarify the goals and expectations for the educational program . . . Once standards are set, teachers can focus and organize their curriculum and instruction to help all students meet standards" (p. 3). The standards, according to Buttram & Waters (1997), can give a great deal of clarity to the process, help to identify the needed resources, and hold everyone accountable for specific outcomes. This prioritization can create a situation where "what gets made into a standard gets done" (p. 3).

The reason standards-based education is significantly different from the prior three innovations is that it falls out of step with the student-oriented innovations of constructivism, user-design, and inquiry-based learning. This movement is motivated much more politically than through research on what is thought to be the best for learning and learners. Standards and accountability are a very politically popular movement. The notion that all learners would reach certain levels of proficiency is laudable, but perhaps not altogether friendly to motivating learning . . . it's more of a stick than a carrot. It also closely prescribes teaching behavior. Lofty (2003) has written of literacy standards, "Because the literacy hour describes what is to be taught, prescribes the means and rigidly allocates the time, the literacy hour arguably restricts teachers' work more than any previous initiative" (p. 203). He argues rather for the definitions of all fields to come from those who are experienced teachers from within disciplines such as English.

Similarly, Kohn (2001) argues that standards and the tests that come with them will disempower teachers and local communities:

> The effect of mandated standards has been not only to control teachers, but to usurp the power of local school districts to chart their own course. If there ever has been a more profoundly undemocratic school reform movement in US educational history than what is taking place in the name of standards, I haven't heard of it. (p. 5)

However, there are plenty of advocates on the other side of the standards question. Wilson (1996) writes,

> There is something certain in a standard. There seems little harm in being certain. Certainty promotes an order that allows us to focus on other issues . . . It is comforting to think we can improve our schools by setting explicit standards for what we want our youth to know and be. (p. 223)

From this perspective, standards can be of great merit for some, particularly politically. Today, the most recent re-incarnation of standards is understood as the CCSS which was launched into development in 2009. The CCSS was developed by the National Governor's Association with input from many other stakeholders, including teachers, with the goal of preparing all students to be career and college ready. CCSS is in part an attempt to standardize across state lines, to ensure that all students in all states are learning the same things and can compete in the job marketplace. The movement is highly political, and there are some difficult conflicts of interest involving companies that created the standards and those same companies that created the tests and also the materials to go with them. Advocates of CCSS point to the freedom schools have to create their own curriculum to meet the standards and they point to the ability of the schools to be able to compare from one state to another and from one country to another to make more complete comparisons.

There are some detractors, naturally, which is almost always the case with a political movement within education. Among the larger concerns is that the current state of schools is not adequate to powerfully apply even the concept of state standards. For example, this is yet another unfunded mandate, after the No Child Left Behind program which has been largely acknowledged as a failure. Concerns raised by detractors include worries that the CCSS might also advance the political agenda to privatize our schools with non-union and market-based schools that will erode the most democratic schools in the world. Some implementations of CCSS have found that the tests to ensure children are thinking critically and not just memorizing material have taken up to 10 hours to complete, and have so fully enveloped the school day that teaching to the test looks good. Some in the business world have even accused the CCSS of producing confusing, frustrating, unhelpful and experimental teaching practices which don't help children do anything except focus on testing with no big picture and no critical thinking—the very things the CCSS was meant to hone. Ultimately, CCSS is so new and untested that it's going to be a while before we know for certain with strong research findings whether the CCSS is going to be useful. There isn't much doubt that it's clearly a part of the larger standards movement and has to be taken seriously despite its many flaws.

Regardless, standards are now a facet of the American education system and are not likely to go anywhere soon. While they may not make a lot of sense within the more learner-centered foci that have emerged from research of the previous 20 years in learning and learning sciences, standards are an important political movement that has taken hold in classrooms all over public schools in America.

### What Are the Components of a Standards-Based Classroom?

- Carefully prescribed content.
- Specific thresholds established for proficient performance at all grade levels.
- State mandated and approved tests.
- Expectations are closely linked to performance.
- All students must be individually checked on all expectations.
- Starts with the standards for the curriculum base.
- Does not specify very much in terms of sequence, activities, or media.
- Outcomes are determined, the means to get there are left open.

Then how is it that we are to utilize the ID4T model in a standards-based classroom? It is quite different actually from either a traditional classroom (the original presentation of the model) or any of the learner-centered classroom approaches. Before approaching the ID4T model in a standards-based classroom, the first step is to determine what phase in the standards process you are faced with. Typically the standards will have already been set. But knowing the general outline of the standards is different from having a complete set of standards explicated by the school board. Are there texts that share the specific standards and what is meant by each of them? (These are often difficult to read tomes.) Have the tests already been set? For the purposes of this illustration we'll assume that the standards are set, the tests are ready, and the outcomes have been explicitly detailed in texts for the teacher. But we'll also assume that the sequence and the means for accomplishing these standards haven't yet been set.

## Set Learning Goals and Objectives

In the standards-based classroom this is usually relatively easy. The standards usually explicate a goal and objectives. Sometimes these goals are not as clear or useful for the classroom as they could be. At times the objectives will not include all the relevant parts (condition, behavior, and criterion) that you'll need. So you'll want to critically review the goals and objectives before using them in your own lesson. Note that one way to tell more precisely what a vaguely worded standard may be asking your learners to accomplish is to carefully check any assessments that are provided to you. You may be able to extrapolate the goal and/or objectives from the assessments.

## Create Authentic Testing

Likewise, it is probable that your tests are already set to meet the standards. The primary problem with the testing in most standards-based programs is that they tend not to be authentic or performance based. This is in direct contrast to the best advice we have from standards experts. Wilson (1996) makes an excellent link to the notion that we should measure performance, which is in clear agreement with the concept that we should align learning and testing: "Standards of learning are not successfully imposed by edict. They are not minimal standards. They are not separate from performance" (p. 24). In the same vein, Ravitch (1995), a pre-eminent expert in standards, writes,

> The customary method of testing in the classroom should be performance assessment, not multiple choice tests. Students should be expected to demonstrate that they can apply what they have learned. Students should know that they will be expected to write essays, perform scientific experiments, engage in debates about historical issues, and exhibit in a variety of ways what they have learned. (p. 183)

Educators need to examine the tests critically and, if they are required tests, be sure to supplement the tests if they are inauthentic or misaligned with the real learning goals and objectives.

### Assess Student Characteristics and Entry Level Behaviors

It will be impossible for learners to accomplish their grade level standards if there are gaps in their past learning or skills that are required before they learn the new skills. Thus, as in past examples, it is essential that care be taken to assure prerequisites are in place in a standards-based classroom. As with inquiry learning, when standards are being used, particularly in high-stakes situations, it is imperative that care be taken to assure that prerequisite skills have been attained and are firmly in place. Pre-tests and surveys are better than more informal methods that may work in traditional, constructivist, or user-design situations.

### Analyze and Select Available Texts

Due to the relatively prescribed nature of standards-based learning, the texts are likely to have already been assigned and pre-determined. However, you may find that the texts are inadequate so do not automatically assume that the assigned text will suffice. Analysis of supplemental texts should follow the same guidelines and heuristics as in the traditional ID4T model.

### Create and Specify Learning Activities and Media

It is unlikely that the activities or media will be pre-specified and if they are it will be important to carefully and critically evaluate whether they will work in your own classroom with your own learners. Assuming that they are not pre-specified you should carefully consider your learning activities and media for novelty, relevance, effectiveness, efficiency, and so forth, in much the same way as you would in the traditional model.

### Plan for Implementation

In the standards-based classroom, administrative support is among the most critical issues associated with implementation. If you are deviating from the prescribed program in any way, it will be important to make these changes clear to the administration and parents as well, particularly to the extent that the standard is a high-stakes standard. Where children's progress to the next grade or high school graduation is on the line, it will be imperative that care be taken with parent communication and administrative support if you are deviating from the provided standards plan in any way. If the standards are not very detailed in their pre-specification of activities and media, it will be important to communicate to parents and administrators what your plan is for reaching those standards. Because of the political nature of standards and the broad nature of implementation planning, planning for implementation in the case of standards will involve extending beyond the classroom to communicate with outside populations.

### Trying Out the Instruction, Evaluating and Revising It

If there is any possibility of trying out the instruction prior to full group implementation, that is definitely advisable. Particularly in the case where you are in a high-stakes testing situation, trying it out with a similar group of learners will have significant benefit and will likely be worth the extra time required in this case. Revising from the trials will follow naturally. Standards do tend to remain the same from year to year (with some unfortunate exceptions) and so if it is not possible or feasible to try out the instruction in a small group prior to full implementation, it will be important to try to look at serious formative evaluation in the first implementation so that the next year will see improved instruction. Formal formative evaluation is preferred if at all possible with surveys, test item analyses, and interviews/group discussions.

Standards are perhaps among the more pervasive innovations taking place in schools today. Using the traditional ID model for the creation of learning in standards-based classrooms takes a few twists and turns. Satchwell & Loepp (2002) conclude that standards should really be about measurement, problem-solving, and communications. They suggest that teachers begin with the standards as a framework for the curriculum and then work through the obstacles and barriers from lack of planning time to facilities, to parent communication, and ask administration for help in that process.

*A Case of ID for Teachers in a*
*Standards-Based Classroom*

Mrs. Sada loved teaching ever since she could remember. Even as a little girl she would line up her dollies and teach them to read. When she did her student teaching she simply fell in love with the experience of teaching 8th and 9th graders. The children were wonderful young people. She found them to be delightful and loved stimulating young minds. Sure, at times they were a little out of line, distant, even defiant at moments, but that was all part of the age. She had learned to accept the changes that her learners went through, and even worked hard to keep up with the latest trends to relate to them, but lately the weight of the No Child Left Behind mandate had been getting her down. What it had meant primarily was a lot more testing for the kids, and in general time spent testing wasn't time spent really working with the kids. Her teaching life was all chopped up into little pieces and this NCLB testing was definitely making that feeling worse. She only saw her students for about an hour (50 minutes to be precise) each day before the bell rang and they moved on to another part of the learning factory to have their geometry or language arts widgets turned. She taught technology to the middle schoolers. But this was a place where there were plenty of standards because 8th grade in particular was the year that technology standards were assessed for NCLB. So she'd decided to focus her attention on one of the standards each month and try to work through what the standards would mean for her classes. She knew that the basic legislation specified that each student needed to be "technologically literate" by the end of 8th grade. And she had learned in the professional development session that this included everyone regardless of race, creed, gender, class, location, or disability. She felt that this last part always went without saying. She sat back down again with the large tome that was the "standards translated"—that's what they called it. It was someone's attempt to specify the standards and how they could be met. But she'd all but thrown the book out at first when she'd tried a few of the lessons and found them to be horribly lacking in almost all areas. Still it was a resource, at least it offered a nice list of the standards for 8th grade. Most of them were simply too broad, she recognized. They said things like "students will master all productivity tools," or "students will demonstrate mastery of technology." That one always got her, well, obviously that was her job, but this broad sort of goal was about all she got from the book in the end.

She focused on one standard that she thought maybe she could make a little more sense of. It was "Students use technology tools to process data and report results." The lesson translation had used the SPSS computer program which was far too advanced a software tool to really work well with this age, she thought, so she scrapped that idea. She had to start from the beginning. OK, she already had the end goal in mind here from the standard (*goal*). She started down the path of which software program to use. At first she thought she might be heading in the wrong direction, specifying the media first. She tended to do that. She suspected it was a hazard of her particular job interest in technology. But then she looked again at the statement—well, it actually said to use technology, but which technology and how? She took a deep breath and forged on with a focus on breaking that rather large goal into more manageable pieces instead of looking at the delivery mode. She knew that there was a lot of work in math on graphing, so she headed down the hall to Mr. Edward's classroom. He was in, also bent over some planning or grading task. They chatted briefly and Mrs. Sada came away with a bit more clarity about what was going on in the math classroom that could help her reach this goal in the latter part of the year. She looked again at the goal and realized it was really two goals: process data and report results. She rewrote the goal as "Students will use technology to report results." She knew that this meant results of prior data processing. Then she broke this large goal into bar graphs, pie charts, and descriptive words and she created learning objectives for each of those (*objectives*). She decided that to really meet this standard she'd need to see her students' final products such as pie charts, bar charts, etc. But given the standard and the goal, perhaps she'd want to see their products as well as their process—how they got the products to the end point. She created a brief rubric that included specific quality check items for the products such as "pie chart accurately reflects data," "bar chart employs appropriate use of

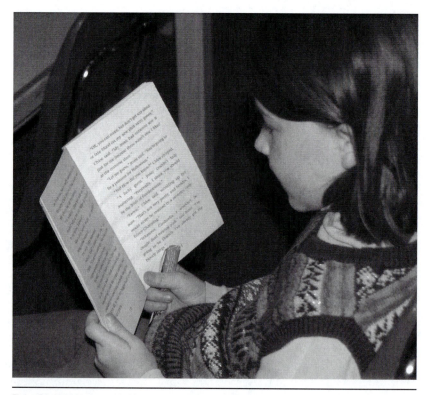

**Figure 7.1** ID4T can be used with traditional standards approaches

color to best reflect results." She also included process items in the rubric, such as "student can open the software and select appropriate tool," or "observed student using technology to build pie chart" (*testing*).

Mrs. Sada knew that the kids had been charting things since kindergarten. Everything from favorite colors to complex data collection in the community had taken place in elementary school. But putting that together with the technology was what this standard was really all about. She thought it might be a good idea to put together a survey to find out what the learners already knew about charting and Excel (her likely choice of technology/media delivery), but decided against it. She simply didn't have the time to get into it. She decided instead to do a quick check with the class orally at the start of the session (*prerequisite*). She knew it wasn't ideal to rely on her informal knowledge of the group for her understanding of learner characteristics and prerequisite levels, but it would have to do this time.

She knew that this standard was covered in the text she was already using in her class, and figured she'd probably use it, but she did review several others to see if they had really good ideas or material that she'd want to use. After reviewing, she landed back with the original text (*text*). Still trying to avoid determining her media specifically but knowing that technology had to be used somehow, Mrs. Sada took some time to specify some activities that she thought would be useful. The students already knew about how to collect data and had been doing so for some years, and they knew (most of them) how to array data in some charts, but none knew how to do this using Excel, which was introduced in her class. She ended up violating a major rule by deciding that she'd use Excel as her media (*media*) prior to deciding precisely what activities she'd use, but those fell quickly into place once she had decided about Excel (*activities*). She had simply no time to try it out with anyone even close to the population, so she simply tried it out in her class live and discovered several issues associated with the technology (*implementation*) and her rubric which she improved (*evaluation/iterative improvement/revision*). In the end, Mrs. Sada felt pretty good about the ways that her skills in ID had helped her navigate the standards.

What You Can Do Now (Chapter Summary)

At this point you will probably be able to:

- Describe what standards-based learning is and its relationship to your own practice and your own classroom.
- List the critical components of the standards-based classroom.
- Explain the ways in which the ID4T model can work with the standards-based classroom.
- Describe a lesson you use that is standards based and how you might work with the ID4T model.

# 8

# Using ID4T in the Online Classroom

## Chapter Questions

1. How can you use ID4T in fully online classrooms?
2. How would ID4T apply to a blended classroom?
3. What are the pros and cons of cybercharter schools?
4. What are the methods of ID4T that might be applied to cybercharters?
5. How does ID4T work in a MOOC?
6. How are online contexts different from traditional classrooms in terms of media selection?
7. What are the special considerations for text selection in online settings?
8. Would you want to teach in an online program? Why/why not or in what type of online setting might you wish to teach?

## What Are the Components of an Online Classroom?

There are many types of online classrooms. Most of us are likely to be familiar with online classrooms that are in the higher education or adult learning settings. Perhaps you have taken an online course for professional development or in your past educational experiences during your teacher preparation. There is a pretty big difference between *taking* such a course in an adult learning setting, and *creating* learning experiences for K-12 learners. We can start by reviewing the different types of online classrooms that you're likely to find out there. For many of you, you'll find that more and more traditional districts are moving toward online blended settings. As we flip classrooms and engage in more learner-centered education, the opportunity to leverage online settings increases. K-12 teaching and learning online (TLO) can include:

- Blended learning (partially online courses) in a traditional classroom.
- Entirely online courses (usually at the high school level) within traditional districts.
- Entirely online schools at the state level within the traditional district.
- Entirely online schools at the state or national level as a cybercharter (independent from traditional school districts).
- Consortia among several entities such as districts, colleges and universities offering entirely online schools.

I would like to specify a few things about cybercharters which are public schools chartered by states, tuition free. Pennsylvania, for example, has several cybercharters and there are some very important financial implications for the traditional public school system as a whole. Charter schools, for those who are unaware, are tuition-free schools chartered by the state and paid for by tuition from the "sending" district (the district or school where the child is currently enrolled prior to enrolling in a charter school). There are "brick and mortar" charter schools with buildings where students attend real-time class sessions and there are cybercharter schools, which are entirely online with potentially a few field trips with others in the school during the year. Many home school families find cybercharters appealing because they provide extensive materials, computer technology (including a stipend for internet connectivity) and curriculum planning—a complete package. But the homeschool student produces a particular issue with the funding as that student wasn't in the system or paid for by the "sending" district and suddenly now *is* being paid for by the sending district. Many of the cybercharters in the United States today are publicly funded by the districts that the student would normally attend, creating problems for the "sending" district. In addition, many of the cybercharters are using those tax dollars for very high-priced curriculum, advertising, and lobbying which may not serve individual learners as well as most of the public would hope.

In addition to concerns about how the taxpayers' monies are being used and the need for careful oversight in cybercharters, everyone obviously wonders whether it works. What evidence do we have that online K-12 learning is effective? After all we're gambling with our children's education, and in some ways the public is gambling with our future as a competitive economy with a civically engaged populace. The research on this topic is *very* difficult to untangle. It is possible to look at the effectiveness across so many different dimensions or variables from student types, course design types, instructional factors and more. In general, the meta studies (that is studies that look at a lot of research studies to determine what research tells us overall) on online K-12 learning seem to indicate that there is little significant difference between online and F2F when variables are controlled for (Cavanaugh & Blomeyer, 2007). However, not all evidence about effectiveness is looking just at individual achievement, some looks to the broader educational enterprise to see if charters (including cybercharters) are good for the *system*. For example, there is compelling evidence that most charter schools (cyber or otherwise) tend to homogenize their student body, meaning that they will often end up with a far less diverse population particularly where race is concerned (Frankenberg, Siegel-Hawley & Wang, 2011). This has created some concern that charter schools really allow families to choose a private-type education and insulate themselves from some of the important social orientation that our schools help our population realize. Understanding K-12 TLO effectiveness is a difficult and unfortunately politically loaded problem. In the end, there is research on both sides of this question that is compelling. Over time, I believe we'll come to a place where we are more certain of the true effectiveness in traditional measures for K-12 TLO. Here are a few hallmarks of K-12 teaching and learning online:

- Tailored for the young learner.
- Highly interactive.
- Requires some live, synchronous teacher time.
- Relies heavily on images, video, audio and far less on text for the young learner.
- K-12 students aged under 12 must have supervision at all times.
- Relies heavily on discussion forums.
- Content is delivered primarily through the internet.

- Students interact with the content on their own, independently (depending on age).
- Can be tailored to the learner needs either by the learner or by the instructor more easily than large traditional classroom delivery.
- Struggles to make certain kinds of learning available online (e.g., science labs, etc.).

Most states are now beginning to establish certificates and endorsements for the online setting in K-12. Most of these certification programs are loosely based on the International Association for K-12 Online Learning (iNACOL) standards. Typically these programs include a field experience in an online setting and require that those in endorsement and certification programs demonstrate knowledge in best teaching practices in online learning, engaging students in powerful ways online, offering regular feedback and appropriate assessment. iNACOL requires, as well, that online instructors model ethical, safe, and legal behavior, can work with diverse and special education populations effectively online, with a deep understanding of a wide variety of approaches, instructional tactics and technologies.

The experience of a teacher who is working in an online K-12 setting represents a significant departure from what most classroom teachers are used to in face-to-face settings. Of particular importance is the advanced design work that has to be done for any online learning experience. Online learning in the K-12 setting does not allow for nearly as many teachable moments as a F2F environment, though there are a few from time to time. Most of the online K-12 learning experience is completely planned out prior to delivery of the instruction. This creates significantly more design demand than might be the case in a F2F setting. The main warning for design in K-12 TLO is *not* to assume that you should replicate what you've done in traditional F2F settings.

### Set Learning Goals and Objectives

This is the first opportunity to move away from using the usual F2F goals and objectives. Take a careful look at the goals and objectives that you have for the session, try to separate yourself from what you may have done in a similar content area in a traditional classroom. However, the process itself is the same. Try to determine, within the limitations and possibilities of what can be done in an online setting, what precisely we want the learner to accomplish. Be careful that you don't set a goal that requires learners to be able to demonstrate something that is beyond the capabilities of the technology of online learning.

### Create Authentic Testing

Naturally, you will still need to align the test items with the goals and objectives. Be sure that your test items don't include things like observation check lists or live demonstrations unless you have some ability to conduct these real-time assessments. Tests in online settings are naturally administered online, but remember that there are so many ways to compromise the "fidelity" of the test—reading the text, checking online for answers, having someone else take the test for you. You should consider how you want to design these assessment *experiences*, not just the test items themselves. Will you have the test administered at a test site where there are proctors? Will you release the learner from the traditional constraints of closed-book testing? How will that impact the robustness of the assessment and your comfort level with the learners' accomplishment of the goals and objectives? These are the critical questions you must answer as you design an assessment for an online administration.

### Assess Student Characteristics and Entry Level Behaviors

In some ways it can be a simpler matter to assess student characteristics and entry-level behaviors online than in the F2F setting because you can easily put together a brief survey or two to determine their learning characteristics and preferences as well as their levels of pre-requisite attainment. In a F2F setting, this administration takes time, but in an online setting, you are likely to get high response rates, anonymity and rapid responses. The only issue here is that you aren't *with* the learners

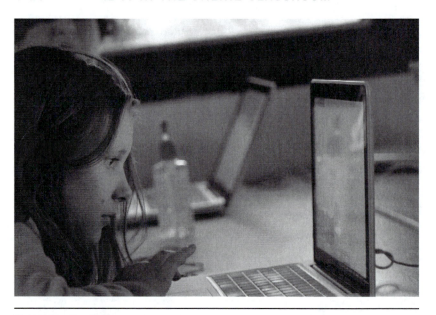

Photo by Jules Carr-Chellman.

and may not have a lot of experience with them and therefore may not know some things about them naturally through exposure to the learners. You may have more trouble making sure that the learners are being honest in their reporting. While this is always the case, of course, the mediated distance of the online setting can increase the likelihood that learners will exaggerate or alter their responses. Therefore some caution should be exercised in how these instruments are administered and analyzed.

### Analyze and Select Available Texts

In this case, the analysis and selection of texts has to be of some great concern. Texts can certainly be traditional book texts, and can be purchased by the learners and studied on their own time, but one may ask whether this takes best advantage of the affordances of the online learning setting. The world is open to the learner on the web and is readily available immediately and often for little or no cost, through the online learning experience. Therefore, it is important to carefully consider what kind of text you wish to use and how you will have your learners access it.

## Create and Specify Learning Activities and Media

Designing effective activities in online learning is typically a significant challenge. Most online courses include discussion forums, content delivered either through video lectures or text, heavy reliance on links beyond the course materials, and heavy reliance on images and graphics. Activities usually ask the learner to engage actively with the content. There are no simple answers to what works in an online course in terms of activities, there are many options and possibilities, but it is important that you carefully consider the potentialities of the online setting. There are so many wonderful opportunities, and replicating what you typically do in the F2F environment is simply limiting and does not do justice to the affordances of the online setting. Media selections in this case are particularly critical. You want to again make sure in activities and media that you are able to vary things as much as possible while taking advantage of the online nature of the learning setting. The primary consideration in making media and activity decisions, then, for online learning is to fully engage the learner using the media at hand online.

## Plan for Implementation

Supports in the implementation of online learning is crucial in a K-12 setting. One of the primary concerns in this case is that the learners, if under the age of 12 in most states, must be supervised. This means that you have a built-in support system at home for at least certain learners. However, it also means that you have to get that partner to "buy in" to the learning goals and expectations. In many cases, online learning will also need extensive support from colleague teachers, administrators, potentially even business managers if the course is part of a cybercharter. It is important to have sufficient supports for getting the materials online if you're not well-versed in doing basic CMS/ LMS development on your own. So design and development support is an important part of the final implementation as well.

## Trying Out the Instruction, Evaluating and Revising It

You'll find this is the area where there are the least specific directives related to the online setting. Trying the instruction out with a small group of learners prior to the large group setting is ideal, but if that's not possible, then piloting the lesson with a large group will still work online. Again, using online surveys and test instruments, as in the case of learner characteristics and prerequisite learning, will be an effective way to determine the effectiveness of the online lesson. Naturally, careful reflection and analysis of findings will help you see both formative and summative data in light of how you can improve the instruction for subsequent offerings.

*A Case of ID for Teaching in an Online Classroom*

Emily Collins had enjoyed teaching English for many years at the high school level. She was deeply engaged in the content. She typically read the great authors and poets during her off time at the beach. Her students thought she was among the most engaging teachers they had at their large suburban high school. The school board had been carefully monitoring the growth of online learning in their district and decided last year to create their own virtual academy. Emily felt it was a good way to reach out to students in a new way. As an early adopter she was among the first to sign up to try to teach online. But she still had her concerns about how the process would work. She found the experience of teaching face-to-face exhilarating and worried that the process of online teaching would be flat and unidimensional. She also worried about her ability to get kids through content in significant and substantive ways, and she found herself worrying a great deal about how to ensure her students would achieve their test scores adequately to prepare them for their college applications—which in this suburb tended toward Ivy Leagues.

She signed up for the virtual academy as one of its first teachers (the school piloted English for 10th graders, basic composition, health, and physical education). She wasn't aware of the process of creating an online course, but at least she knew the kinds of things that needed to go into the course and what her goals were based on her face-to-face experiences.

Her first meeting with a district instructional designer/production manager to help her create the course was an eye opener. They laid out a process for creating the course, which included goal and objective setting, "content dumps," activity selection and media production. The process itself felt very different to her than how she had planned her face-to-face courses for years. Usually she would simply lay out a plan, have a goal in mind, possibly create a rubric or two to help with the largely subjective assessments of students' writing and then put together daily plans for each section. But the daily experiences unfolded more than were prescribed and the online planning had to be done entirely in advance.

Emily spent several days scoping out the entire course and laying out goals and objectives (*goals and objectives*). The process took much longer than she'd expected but was good in terms of seeing the entire course at a high level and knowing where the course was headed, as well as what she hoped to expect of her learners at the end of the course. She started with her goals and objectives and broke them down completely. Having run those by the instructional designer, who refined them slightly, catching a few errors in verbiage and compound objectives, she revisited the question of what her learners already knew and what she felt she could count on in terms of prerequisite learning (*entry level skills*). At that point, the course went into "production."

Emily was encouraged to move to content dumps and figuring out the activities (*activities*). She knew that the alignment was important, and she opted to start with the rubrics for assessments based on her goals and objectives. She at first relied too heavily on the rubrics she'd used for years (*test items*). She realized that her goals had changed slightly, and had to take some time to backtrack, revisit the objectives and move toward rubrics that were aligned and that were far more explanatory and clear than her previous rubrics. She realized that the online learner wasn't going to have the benefit of daily contact with her to help clarify expectations, and this helped to color her work as she created the content and activities as well. They were far expanded from her notes. Not lectures, but a lot of text.

Her instructional designer recognized that some work needed to be done now that the activities were aligned with objectives and test items/rubrics along with activities and content, to begin the process of integrating appropriate media (*media*). The instructional designer met with Emily and suggested several options including some interface ideas, uses of some innovative media like videos, wiki spaces and timeline interfaces. After decisions were made with the instructional designer, the production team went to work helping her to create the lessons one by one and getting her approval on each one. She felt very fortunate to be a part of the pilot as well as being housed in a relatively well-off district where resources were devoted to the online virtual academy's development.

When the time finally arrived to launch the course (there was no opportunity to try the materials out with smaller groups, it was sink or swim with the course as it was designed) her instructional designer did assure her that it would be possible to make changes for the next offering and encouraged her to keep track of her suggested changes (*formative evaluation*). The experience itself was a truly mixed bag for Emily, who felt disconnected from her learners, but also recognized the joy of working with students that she couldn't reach effectively otherwise. Her class included an Olympic athlete, a shy girl who had been bullied, and an international student whose family had recently moved to the States and whose conversational English was weak, but whose writing was exemplary.

It was an exciting and exhausting experience for her, and helped her to see the value of the virtual academy. At the conclusion of the course, she asked if she could speak with some of the students beyond the basic student satisfaction survey to get more texture to their experiences. She learned about some of the technical glitches particularly, and realized she would have to be more attentive to job aids for her learners to make sure their experiences with the interfaces, some of which were quite new to the students, were positive and productive. In the end, the pilot was successful and both teachers and learners found the process of learning online to be highly enriching.

**What You Can Do Now (Chapter Summary)**

At this point you will probably be able to:

- Describe what online learning is and its relationship to your own practice and your own classroom.
- List the critical components of the online classroom.

- Explain the ways in which the ID4T model can work inside an online classroom.
- Distinguish between online learner needs and face-to-face learner needs.
- Apply these distinctions to the design of an online lesson.

# 9

# USING ID4T IN THE FLIPPED CLASSROOM

**Chapter Questions**

1. How can you use ID4T in flipped classrooms?
2. What are the pros and cons of flipped classrooms?
4. What are the methods of ID4T that might be applied to flipped classrooms?
5. How are flipped classrooms different from traditional classrooms in terms of media selection?
7. What are the special considerations for text selection in flipped classrooms?
8. Would you want to transform your own classroom into a flipped classroom? Why/why not?

**What Is a Flipped Classroom?**

The flipped classroom is a slightly different take on how we organize *time* within the classroom. The basic outline of a flipped classroom is that we take the tasks that we normally do during the school day and ask the learner to do them during homework time (at night, at study hall, or at home). Then what we had traditionally thought of as the homework tasks are done in class as guided practice. Math is the most common and easily understood of these examples. With the help of Khan Academy tools, almost all math skills are easily reviewed and introduced with videos online. Thus, a learner might be asked to watch a video on two-digit multiplication with carrying online and given a link emailed home to the parents indicating this is their homework. Or they may be asked to watch a video their teacher prepared targeting a specific similar skill. That is their homework, which would typically have been presented during class time. Then the practice session, which would have normally been given as homework, is offered as an in-class experience with guidance from the instructor. In this way, standard presentations, where not all that much interaction actually happens, is relegated to home while the teacher is able to really connect with learners over their struggles with doing practice sets of problems.

Please understand this is not really a new idea at all. Rather, the flipped classroom is informed by the proposals through the centuries from the Socratic method to John Dewey to Maria Montesorri. It is important that we understand learning is something that happens for children in spite of rather than because of our best efforts. The Boy Scouts is perhaps a great example of flipped classrooms that have taught boys many high-risk training skills such as shooting arrows and guns, building fires, and throwing tomahawks. They have materials that have to be studied, videos are sometimes involved, but more commonly the scout learns from a workbook on their own first, then they come to a meeting and *do* the activity they've been studying. They are guided by scout masters and older experienced scouts (peer teaching and leadership) and they have had great success with such a model—low tech as it is.

In some ways, given modern technology, the flipped classroom makes a lot of sense. It allows us to avoid problems such as parents not being available to help their children with their homework, and it creates a much more student-centered learning environment in the classroom, with the teacher coaching rather than presenting. It also allows the teacher more contact in some ways as their homework and classwork are all being impacted by the instructor (depending on how the videos are selected and produced). But in some other ways, this approach is fraught with issues. Perhaps the most obvious problem is what we do for learners with no or slow Internet access. Video bandwidth is greedy and very slow if the access points are not high speed. This could create an even wider digital divide among those who do and those who don't have the resources for good connectivity and the necessary technology at home to do their homework. And while some flipped classrooms also incorporate online discussions and peer questioning, in general, the learner is left on their own to learn new content without direct interaction with the teacher, and that can be a bit difficult for the learner. On the other hand, those teachers who do make themselves available to help, admirable as that is, also open a different door—24/7 access to teachers and extending far beyond their normal expectations and union-negotiated contract requirements. In essence, is the teacher taking on, for no additional pay, the duty of essentially getting the learners through their homework as well as their classwork?

The availability of online video tools is one of the primary reasons that flipped classrooms are taking off. However, good video is expensive and difficult to produce. While it is certainly possible to create a video of a teacher talking about a subject, and even demonstrating something, the video quality may be difficult for the learners to learn from if it is not of relatively high quality. It reminds me of one of those sayings doctors have when faced with whether or not to give a patient with an advanced disease yet another treatment, "Just because you *can* do something doesn't mean you *should*." In this case we need to carefully examine whether what we are offering the learner for their online work is of sufficient quality to engage them in learning the content and whether their activities within class are also sufficiently engaging. From an instructional design standpoint, the notion of a flipped classroom is not an anathema. It can definitely work, but as usual, we must start with the beginning steps of learning goals and objectives.

While current indicators of success in schools suggest that we may need to find an alternative such as flipping classrooms, research hasn't strongly indicated universal success of the flipped approach either. We need to have some critical understandings of the impacts of flipped classrooms from the research as well. The ASCD website (www.ascd.org/publications/educational-leadership/mar13/vol70/num06/Evidence-on-Flipped-Classrooms-Is-Still-Coming-In.aspx) indicates that more research is indeed needed to support strong flipped classrooms. Some self-report surveys show that flipped classrooms are taking off with lots of teachers trying it, but little real achievement research is yet available to tell us whether the method is working. What little research we have is equally positive and negative in terms of its findings, with some classrooms reporting increased scores on tests, while others indicate decreases. From this perspective the jury is still out on the widespread uses of flipped classrooms. However, the potential for self-paced learning, learner control, and learner-centered instruction are compelling and worth at least examining how we engage in ID for the flipped classroom.

### Set Learning Goals and Objectives

As with any form of instruction, the flipped classroom starts with a clear learning goal and supporting objectives. Really, this step will not change appreciably in the flipped classroom since the primary innovation here is related to the way that *time* is used in the delivery of instruction rather than what we hope the learner will be able to do at the end. Too often we forget to start with the end in mind, so even in a flipped classroom we will first specify the learning outcomes by setting the goals and objectives.

### Create Authentic Testing

Again, very little will likely change in the testing area. Naturally, all tests must be aligned with the learning goals. In all likelihood these will include standardized testing. The one area that can cause some issues with flipped classrooms in the assessment area is that teachers have a bit more of a close-up view on their learners' daily abilities to actually *pass* the tests they're going to be taking. Because the teacher sees the learners every day as they work through what had been homework, the teacher may have a keener sense in a flipped classroom of what their learners are capable of. This could cause the teacher to change test items to better align with what learners are capable of. This should really not be considered, as the purpose of assessment in a flipped classroom (as in most standard classrooms) is to determine the ability of the learners to demonstrate mastery of the material. Tests must be designed before instruction commences and they should remain stable.

### Assess Student Characteristics and Entry Level Behaviors

Here we will probably see a large difference between a flipped classroom and a traditional classroom. First, we need to determine for sure that learners have access to the necessary equipment and materials (online videos most of the time) to actually *receive* the instruction during off-school hours. In some cases, this access will rely on libraries (in which there are limited numbers of computers and sometimes long waits and short time limits on use) or after-school programs (which can add costs). It is essential in a flipped classroom that before the instruction is moved to a flipped format, the learners' access is fully analyzed.

As an instructional designer, you'll still want to assess the other related characteristics, with special attention to the ability of your learners to sustain interest in the videos presented. You may also need to carefully consider whether you have learners who may have problems with listening to the videos for a long time. Do you need to have special accommodations for blind or hearing-impaired learners or ADHD students? Or are there other considerations for your student body that may make flipping your classroom a problem? Consider them all during this step.

Your entry-level behaviors are likely to be similar to the typical analysis you would do, where you break down the objectives into sub- and sub-sub-objectives, to a point where you come to an entry-level behavior. So the process for this is not really likely to differ substantially, except that you should also track individual differences within this analysis. If you know that you have some learners with certain levels of entry behavior, you may need to consider whether flipping your classroom will work. Individual differences within your classroom mean that we often have to present something in multiple ways. Doing so within a flipped classroom is far less likely (typically a video presents a topic or skill one way and leaves it) than if a teacher stands before her class and realizes that half her learners don't "get it" by their non-verbal cues. So paying close attention to individual differences within this step of analysis will avoid significant problems later in the instructional implementation.

### Analyze and Select Available Texts

Texts in flipped classrooms are more likely to have significant impact on the learning than in traditional classrooms. In a flipped classroom, one can easily imagine a learner, confused by the video or finding that something is unclear, relying much more heavily on the textbook for *explanations* than merely or primarily for sample exercises, which will be covered in the classroom itself. Therefore, the texts you select in a flipped classroom must be expository in clear and simple ways that will speak to learners. Some special effects such as motivational colors may be less important than the clarity of the text itself. Learners are more likely to be motivated to engage the text because of their own confusion and won't need cartoon characters to draw them in, they'll have real work they want to get done and understanding will be a motivator in itself. In addition, any text that has accompanying videos will be highly prized because if they are well developed, highly produced and clear, they will represent a very important resource for a flipped classroom teacher. Thus, text selection will be affected by the flipped classroom innovation in substantive ways.

### Create and Specify Learning Activities and Media

Obviously, the activities and media selection step in the ID process is perhaps the most impacted by a decision to move to a flipped classroom model. This innovation asks us to use time very differently and it has a huge impact on what we do in terms of activities and media. In most cases, video lectures will be a cornerstone of the new flipped classroom instructional design. Once it has been determined that the learners lend themselves to flipped classroom administration, and that the learners have the ability to access the materials online, and that you have accommodated individual differences, the selection process can begin. Identifying appropriate videos or creating your own is a time-consuming process, and remember that media should be engaging and motivating to your learners. Most flipped classrooms rely heavily on videos presented online to the learners in their home as part of their homework. This is a good place to begin, with this assumption. However, materials could also be presented via online texts, or off line texts, simulations, or games. These materials are typically supported with discussions and teacher/student or student/student interactions during the time the learner is working on their own to understand content. In this case, flipping the classroom will have fairly dramatic impacts on the activities and media selected. Care should be exercised to align activities not only with the flipped nature of the desired final classroom, but also with the learning goals/objectives *and* the inherent media affordances of those media selected to deliver instruction.

### Plan for Implementation

Implementation for any innovation that is a significant departure from tradition is of great concern for the instructional designer in a K-12 setting. The politics and context can and will exert a great deal of pressure on the innovator. In general, large systems, like schools, tend to have a sense of momentum in a given, traditional, direction. Deviation from this direction will draw attention and those who may be uncomfortable for many reasons will likely try to encourage more traditional, familiar choices. In the case of the flipped classroom, it is clear that there are some easy targets for political attacks—the nature of the school day, and time demands on teachers is a good example. You should be sure to plan carefully for any flipped classroom implementation. Make sure that you have clearly aligned the needed supports from administration and fellow teachers whenever possible. Parent and even community communication will be essential. Have a local news reporter let the community know as you are implementing, and while you're in the planning stages, make sure to send plenty of communications home to parents so they'll understand that this is a very different approach and one that will require their support to ensure their children get the content presentation that they need at home. There may be other needed supports that go far beyond your own personal space, such as having an afterschool program or expanded time limits at your public library to ensure access. All of these concerns must be carefully examined and planned for prior to implementation.

### Trying Out the Instruction, Evaluating and Revising It

Naturally, as you try out the flipped classroom for the first time, it's likely to have lots of fixes that are needed and large revisions. One thing to carefully consider is the possibility of having smaller trials prior to full implementation. This allows you to see how well students of various abilities and individual differences may respond to your designed flipped classroom. So it may be more important than in traditional classroom settings that you spend some time trying out the basic flipped classroom design with small groups in your classroom before a full implementation. You should collect similar data to traditional ID4T data for evaluation purposes—both formative and summative.

*A Case of ID for Teaching in a Flipped Classroom*

Miss Lindy had taught fourth grade for going on 20 years and loved it. She loved the kids and the excitement of working with young minds. She always felt that they were, by 4th grade, able to be sufficiently mature to really handle tough content, but also young enough to be excited by every new discovery.

Miss Lindy attended a seminar on flipped classrooms sponsored by the principal in her elementary school. The seminar was not all that well attended, which had sort of surprised Miss Lindy, since she thought the *idea* of flipped classrooms was interesting. Some of the content in the session had surprised her, but overall she had gone into the session having at least a sense of what the flipped classroom was about. She knew that it meant she would have to create a fair bit of content, but she was excited about the opportunity to do homework with the kids. She knew some other teachers weren't so thrilled about that, and wanted to leave it to the parents, but she felt that homework was so variable because some parents were deeply engaged in (maybe even too deeply engaged in) helping their kids do their homework, while others ignored it, or worse, scheduled too many afterschool activities to allow their kids to really get to their homework effectively. She worried about whether all of her learners would have access to the materials, but the school was in a relatively well-off neighbourhood and she had some level of confidence going into the experience that most of the learners would be likely to have adequate access. After the seminar she knew she'd have to get a survey out there to make *sure* that they'd have access before committing too far to flipping her classroom.

She started to organize some resources with this in mind, and decided to focus on math for her first flipped experience. While she

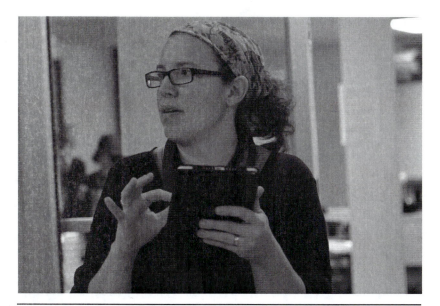

Photo by Jules Carr-Chellman.

was sure other areas would also lend themselves to flipping, she thought math might be a good first target. She felt that knowing how the kids were doing on what she still thought of as their traditional homework, which would now be done under her watchful eye, would help her ensure her children were ready for standardized tests. She also was taken with the Khan Academy resources for 4th grade in this area and decided to focus on math for flipping. She reviewed her goals and objectives from the previous year and none of them needed to change. She then looked at the test items, again no changes there, they were all well aligned already and standardized, so she moved on to the next step in the ID4T model. Here she knew she had to send home a survey as well as some early communication about her plan to flip her classroom. She organized a note along with a brief survey to ensure she was looking for all necessary accommodations for her learners as well as recognizing their access issues. She then went through the usual process of determining their entry-level skills, which had for years included a brief pre-test in math, and she decided to specifically focus on double-digit multiplication (with division to follow if multiplication worked well). This was an area that really did extend prior learning, and Miss Lindy wanted to try the flipped classroom not with an area that was a review of prior learning, but something that really built on prior learning and began new learning skills.

Miss Lindy then turned her attention to selecting texts and activities. She decided that her current text wasn't sufficiently clear and she knew there were trouble spots in the book where her learners routinely struggled. They were smack in the middle of the area she intended to focus on, and so she reviewed several other texts and with a flipped classroom in mind, she selected an alternative text for at least the section on two-digit multiplication. She reviewed some guides on flipped classrooms so she'd have a better understanding of guided practice sessions and what her classroom would look like as well as what her student's homework online experiences would look like. She also selected two Khan videos that she thought would work, but felt she should do a video introduction as well as two brief alternative presentations. Based on her years of experience presenting this material, she felt that most learners would likely get the basics from Khan, but there were some learners she suspected would need a different approach, so she videotaped herself using a very simple set up with a tripod and her cell phone, and a white board behind her. While the production values were weak, the basics were there and she felt satisfied with what she had in terms of materials for home. Miss Lindy worried that perhaps she should have considered other media, such as text-based or simulation-based activities that media might work well with, but determined that such an approach was out of alignment with her goals and overall activities. She then turned her attention to planning for the session at school and determined that she might like to have slightly modified, and in some ways more challenging practice problems as she knew she'd be present to help the learners with them. Having revamped the activities and texts, she felt ready for the next phase . . . dealing with the politics!

She looked at the overall problem of implementing the flipped classroom in her school. She felt pretty confident that her parents and junior teachers would support her. And the building principal was fully supportive, having sponsored the seminar where she first got the idea to try out flipped classrooms. So part of the battle was already won. But she was very concerned about union issues and concerns voiced by some of the more senior faculty during that seminar she had attended. It seemed as though some of them had come just to complain or put up roadblocks that she hoped wouldn't turn up in her own implementation. She knew she had to prepare just in case other teachers or the union created any stir about it. She looked carefully at the union contract to be sure that she could do the flipped classroom experience within the confines of the contract. She recognized that she would be doing some "teaching" during the evenings as she interacted with students in an online discussion forum. But she wouldn't be grading papers at home, and she felt that a fair trade-off in terms of time. She did decide she would limit her time online to specific hours, which she would let the parents know about, so she wouldn't feel on call 24/7.

To shore up her support, she spoke to several junior teachers about her plan as well as her principal to ensure there was sufficient openness to others about the new plan. A more senior teacher got wind of her plans and did approach her after school one day in her classroom. "I'm not sure this is such a great idea, have you really thought this through?" Mr. Harvey had asked. A debate ensued between the two of them, with Mr. Harvey pointing out that there was going to be a lot more of her time demanded, that parents might be confused, and that the students might come to expect this form of time structure. He also argued that there was little substantive research that showed that it worked, and wondered why she would, "venture out into uncharted territory without research that proved it was all worth it." While Miss Lindy wasn't sure she had actually convinced Mr. Harvey, she did feel that she had calmed his biggest concerns and had continuously let him know that this was a trial for now, and not something that was going to be forced on others at present. This seemed to help at least a little, but she realized that she had better make sure parents were well-informed, as many of the senior teachers were friends with influential parents and she wanted to avoid a political rebuff of the flipping if possible.

She also tried the materials out with her three nephews who were 3rd and 4th graders from her two sisters' families. This small trial worked very well, she was very excited that it had worked as well as it had, but had a few minor adjustments to make, particularly pointing to specific spots in the text that would help slower learners understand the videos. She found that the extra videos were useful, but for two of her three learners it had been a waste of time to review different ways to understand two-digit multiplication. She decided to allow these other videos to stand as "optional" in case a learner didn't feel they understood the content at the end of the Khan videos. She collected not only some test analysis from her trial group, but also talked to them about what they thought of the experience, and got some additional feedback that she implemented along with some good quotes to use in her letter home to parents about how kids felt about the instruction.

The day came and she implemented the lessons over a period of two weeks and found that the learners responded very well. She still had to do some "traditional" classroom teaching. She answered the same question multiple times while students worked on the guided practice, and realized that she probably should clarify something that they were mostly misunderstanding. Two of her students hadn't watched the videos at all and were very confused. She had to set them aside to watch on their own, but she emphasized that it was imperative that they get to their homework consistently. She sent a quick email home to both sets of parents emphasizing this as well, and didn't have a repeat problem in subsequent lessons that used the flipped model. Miss Lindy used a number of evaluative methods to examine the effectiveness of the lesson from both formative and summative standpoints. She started looking at the summative questions—was the lesson worth running in this way, should she do it again in future years or even future units this year? She determined that although the politics were a little scary, overall the effect *had* been good and she would repeat. She then turned to the formative evaluation data and determined that several things needed to change in future implementations of the lesson or any other flipped lessons, with even more communications with parents needed. In the end, she thought she'd do it again, but didn't feel it would be good for every content area. In particular, she was loath to give up her read alouds with the class, they had been reading *Mr. Popper's Penguins* and she did not want to do *that* on video. She did all kinds of voices and actions when she read aloud and loved the spontaneous nature of it, but didn't fancy having her acting immortalized on video. She felt great about her first foray into flipping her classroom and also felt that the ID4T model had worked pretty well to guide her through that process.

**What You Can Do Now (Chapter Summary)**

At this point you will probably be able to:

- Identify the pros and cons of flipping your classroom.
- List the kinds of special considerations you must make in ID4T processes if you flip your classroom.
- Determine your own interest in flipping your classroom.
- Tailor your ID4T design to fit a flipped classroom.

# 10
# GAMING AND ID4T

## Chapter Questions

1. How can you use games and ID4T to improve your classroom?
2. What are the possible applications of gaming in classrooms?
4. What are the methods of ID4T that are best applied to a gaming classroom?
5. How are gaming classrooms different from traditional classrooms in terms of media selection?
7. What are the special considerations for text selection in gaming classrooms?
8. Do you want to use games in your classroom? Why/why not? What sorts of games?

## What Is all This Fuss about Games for Learning?

People have been playing games forever. From the time that leisure came to the human race, games have been a part of what we are about. Even in isolated cultures with no technology, we see inventive games created by children and adults to pass the time in fun, competitive ways. Games have been around forever, there's really nothing at all new about them. And using games to learn has been around almost as long as entertainment games ... in fact it can be argued that gaming *is* learning at almost any level. While some of you may be dismissing what I'm suggesting here as rubbish, believing that games and fun things are fundamentally non-educative, I'd challenge you to think about the last game you played. Was it a board game? A role play? A computer game? A video game? A party game? All are great examples of fun, entertaining, but also learning games. Think back, what did you do in the game? And if you failed at the first attempt, did you change your approach for the second attempt? And if you did that, can you really say that you did not learn?

While you may recognize that games *are* in fact powerful learning engines, do you still resist their integration (particularly video games) into the classroom? Why? Study your answer to this question. If you see that video games, like other games, teach real skills, why would we want to ban them from classrooms? Is it because some of them have fantasy violence? Or because they tend to be highly gendered so only some kids will play some games and others won't? Or is it because they focus on individual achievement and competition rather than the model of collaborative classrooms we often strive for? Is it most of all because it feels like you don't have time for it, and it takes away from other pressing (standardized test prep) matters in your classroom? Is it all of these reasons and more? We could walk away now, end this chapter by throwing in the towel, but I challenge you to re-think that position. Rather than rejecting gaming as nonsense or too much sugar to get the medicine down, think instead of the powerful opportunities that gaming can unleash.

First, what is the most important factor in an effective long-lasting education? It is not the presence of high technology, alternative methods of teaching, learner-centered classrooms, or high-stakes testing. None of these are the best predictor of effective educative experiences. The key is absolutely a caring teacher. Having a caring teacher in the lives of learners has proven time and again to be the most compelling factor in effective learning experiences in the classroom. Believe it or not, I feel that games unlock this caring connection in ways that almost nothing else will in classrooms. Games are not the domain of most teachers. In fact, very few teachers play games of any sort on a regular basis, even fewer play video games, even social ones like words with friends, and even fewer (almost none) play competitive violent video games, thought of as serious games, like *World of Warcraft* (WoW) or *Call of Duty* (CoD). Games like these are the domain of kids, and often boys who we seem to be losing at record-breaking speed. We have alienated so many learners with our coercive learning models, that we simply need to re-engage and one way is to honor the things that matter to them.

I'm not suggesting that we simply give in and let the kids do whatever they feel like, or that we should glorify violence or war. I'm not suggesting that only the boys get this good connection with teachers through gaming. Not at all. I believe that using games as a curricular material has the potential to be a powerful learning tool that *also* allows a deep caring connection with a teacher. We honor their culture, and at the same time we ask the learners to help us learn what they already know about a game.

There is ample evidence that learning is occurring in gaming, even video gaming, and that this learning can include transfer to traditional learning settings in history, physics, math, and language. Games can build strong leaders, and strong followers. Games tend to create excellent communication skills, and strong problem-solving skills as well as critical thinking and grit or perseverance. Games teach kids to learn from mistakes rather than that they are failures when they fail. Games are not a panacea, however—there are plenty of problems with games in the classroom, not the least of which is that there is a good deal of time involved in teachers learning how to *play* much less *use* games to good effect. But when time is appropriately invested and teachers learn games from kids, a strong bond can form from respect and learning together.

## *A Word on Gamification*

Gamification is the process of taking a (usually) relatively mundane task and making it more appealing, fun, entertaining and motivating by adding gaming elements. The well-known game advocate Jane McGonigal suggests that school should become a game. Instead of grades we have levels, and you earn points for learning things that can earn you various things of value in the game. I've tried this kind of gamification in the past ... even asking my kids to do laundry by giving them certain aspects of game mechanics. While I think there are benefits to this kind of hyped-up token economy, we do have some pretty compelling evidence that suggests that internal motivation over time is much more effective in creating whole, productive, purpose-led people. Extrinsic rewards, which seem more evident in the gamification than they do in gaming itself, can be damaging to long-term motivation for humans. Games themselves, however, are not the same thing. As with educational games, kids know when they're being manipulated into learning something. They want to learn what they want to learn and not by being tricked into it. Coercive learning really doesn't work (Kohn, 2001). Instead we should be very cautious and potentially very smart about any gamification we attempt in learning situations. First, honesty can be a hallmark of gamification to make it clear that you know what gamification is, and that this isn't a trick, it's something we're all doing together for fun. Overdoing gamification can create frustration and alienation—the opposite of the goals for using games effectively in the classroom. So subtle, honest uses of some of these token economies, along with a clear understanding of the limits of external motivators, may be somewhat useful. To me, gamification along with educational games, have very limited applications and effectiveness.

*A Caution*

As with any ID lesson, the process seems quite linear, but as we all already know it's much more iterative and circular. In the case of gaming application to learning, we have to assume an activity, approach, and media have been determined *prior* to the steps of objectives, goals, tests, etc. This is completely backward from all that we've learned to this point about how to do ID4T. Rather than starting out with a plan to integrate games, the best approach is to have games make sense within the normal flow of ID4T design processes. However, in some cases, you may find that your learners are disengaged, and that the best way to reach them will be by using a game that they're playing. You may watch some play and discover a clear link to a curricular goal you have. This is a more iterative approach, back and forth between the steps. But it takes good advantage of opportunities and teachable moments in ways that transcend slavish adoption of ID4T. As you explore the steps below, please be sure to carefully read the case with this chapter's materials, as that will help to show a sensible application of gaming to an ID4T design process.

What can we do with games in the classroom? There are a wide variety of possibilities from board games to role plays to video games. ID4T can guide us through the maze of many options among gaming as a curricular material and help to establish productive and powerful uses of games in traditional classrooms.

### Set Learning Goals and Objectives

Games can be used in traditional learning, and the goals and objectives really should not be significantly affected. As always, goals and objectives must be carefully identified with the same due diligence that is needed for any ID.

### Create Authentic Testing

Again, very little will likely change in the testing area. Naturally, all tests must be aligned with the learning goals. In all likelihood these will include standardized testing. The primary benefit of games in classrooms is a recognition of the amazing value of learning from mistakes. This represents a significant departure from traditional testing. One way to capitalize on this benefit is to focus on in-game accomplishments rather than one-and-done test scores. Game success, however, does need to translate to traditional test outcomes at some point, and so integrating games into a lesson may or may not affect the testing or assessment design significantly.

### Assess Student Characteristics and Entry Level Behaviors

This is a step in the ID process that will show a fair amount of change from the traditional classroom. Here it becomes very important that you know for sure that your learners are able to access games either on mobile devices or on gaming systems. Games should *not* further the digital divide, but we also have to be cautious that they don't exacerbate the gender differences in classrooms either. Boys are more likely to be playing games that will fit into the deep thinking category, and girls are more likely to be playing social games like Farmville. Each may have their proper place in the curriculum and depending on what you're designing for (what your goal is) you may want to use either, but don't allow overly gendered games to create a rift between the genders in your classroom. Assess the extent to which boys are willing to play "girl" games, and vice versa to ensure their individual gender differences won't get in the way of their achievement of your overall learning goal. Other than these sensitivities, this step would proceed as usual with proper surveys and analysis of the learning objectives to the prerequisite levels.

### Analyze and Select Available Texts

Selecting texts for a class where games are likely to be used won't differ all that much from selecting texts otherwise. The text should, as in the flipped classroom, embody clarity in case the game itself misses some aspects of learning that you want the learner to get through engagement with the selected texts. So you may heighten your attention to clear explanations in texts in a gaming class design. You may also want to include game texts themselves. Readily available online, most games have a variety of text materials available that most gamers use routinely. The access to various "cheats" online is a well-known practice in gaming circles, and having a clear image of how those online texts and videos fit into a design for a gaming classroom will be an important part of the selecting texts step.

### Create and Specify Learning Activities and Media

Here you'll be spending a good deal of time fleshing out the use of the gaming solution, assuming that you decided after the previous steps that you still want to use games in your classroom for that particular learning goal. Activities can range from playing the game at home and unpacking what was learned the next day in class, to discussing the game without actually playing it, to playing it in class together, in groups or individually with think-aloud or dialogue about learning that is happening while game play is ongoing. Thus, while gaming may seem like a simple media choice that will also drive your activities, it is possible to utilize games in a wide variety of ways and they should all be carefully considered in light of the learning goal during this step.

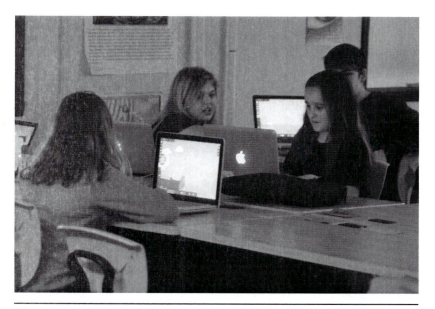

Photo by Jules Carr-Chellman.

## Plan for Implementation

One of the more difficult things for teachers to adjust to when using games in the classroom is the nature of deep, engaging games. Serious games, as they're often called, take huge swaths of time to experience. For a teacher who has never had any interest in this kind of gaming, using games to good effect in the classroom is fraught with potholes from time management to equipment management. Perhaps even more daunting, most parents and administrators will heavily question involvement with violent video games, no matter how "fantasy" the violence portrayed is. Even when following the guidelines for game age, teachers can easily get in trouble from parents who are blinded by media portrayals of gamers as Columbine shooters. This can be said of board of education members and administrators as well . . . and lots of fellow teachers. In some ways, really taking kids where they are with the games they already play, to show them all the wonderful things they're learning and to help them make translations to their own learning, can create a stir in almost any school. Planning for this level of political cover and implementation is serious business and must be approached as early in the process as possible. It is so disappointing to see a great plan, to integrate the materials and games, and then to have the district say "no" because there is too high a level of discomfort with kids killing zombie sheep and pigs in Minecraft. So do your homework as early as you can to determine the political openness to having games in the classroom. In many ways you should do this step first if you can—to think about implementation first does seem a bit off, but it can save you a lot of time and track you into using the ID4T model from another option such as standards or flipped classrooms, if you know up front.

If your district *is* accepting and encouraging your efforts to integrate games, congratulations! Now you will need to be sure you have very clear information being communicated to your parents and fellow teachers. That is imperative in the case of gaming, which tends to be underestimated as educational material. In addition to preparing for the politics and communication, be certain that your logistics are in order, that you are prepared to use games with proper technology, and support.

### Trying Out the Instruction, Evaluating and Revising It

This step is very similar to traditional ID4T, though you'll have to pay special attention to the questions of summative evaluation as it is important that you have clear indicators as to whether it makes sense to use games again in the future or not. If your data tells you "no" accept that answer, but if you have support for gaming, it can be very powerful in persuading other teachers, parents, and administrators that using games to support learning has significant positive payoffs.

### *A Case of ID4T in a Gaming Classroom*

Mrs. Robinson had taught in urban settings her whole career, but two years ago, when the opportunity to engage in the founding of a charter school aimed at re-engaging boys at the elementary level came up, she knew she'd found her calling. Working in the poorest neighborhood in Washington DC, the school was formed specifically to find innovative ways to get young men to reach literacy at all levels and start them off on the right foot educationally. The school was intentionally small, and what made the news was that it was a single-gender school. Mrs. Robinson wasn't totally sure that this was for the best. Seeing how girls and boys learn from each other had given her lots of good insights into each gender, but she knew that the real problems in learning at this point were far more among the boys than the girls. She saw that the girls were able and willing to sit still and do their work more diligently, so they did well overall in school, but the boys—oh the boys! In her years of teaching she saw more boys slip through her fingers with poor achievement and even poorer grades. She saw boys who had tuned out of traditional school by 2nd grade and she was desperate to somehow engage them in caring and serious ways.

She was assigned to teach 2nd grade in the new school and hoped she'd be able to find ways to relate to them as a caring teacher that would engage them wholly in their education. She started the school year full of hope and promise and watched them carefully. Mrs. Robinson had always believed in "taking kids where they are" and the early fall found her taking lots of time to talk to the kids and find out what really interested them. She quickly came to the conclusion that the boys all played video games for hours each week and loved to play them and to talk about playing them.

Not being all that experienced with gaming, she started by asking the boys to bring in some games and show her what they were all about, to write about games, and to talk with her some more about what they did with games. However, she did this without really thinking through some of the implications of this open invitation. Games that were rated "M" for mature, and were overly violent (in her view) came streaming into the classroom, they were talked about, written about and shown. The parents and administrators got wind of the goings-on and promptly shut her down, citing too much violence and inappropriate materials for some of the boys who weren't exposed to such games at home. Mrs. Robinson did a good job of combatting the concerns and pointing to the natural development of boys' violent fantasy lives, but nothing she said would convince parents that an "M" game in a 2nd grade was OK. She backed down, but four months later, she saw a perfect entrée for *Minecraft* in her second grade classroom and began working on her plan to put it into place with care and open communication.

She had several goals related to math, in particular the beginnings of area and was used to using manipulative blocks for this, but she realized that using *Minecraft* would be much more exciting and could integrate several other things that were planned for later in the school year. She believed it would be a useful media choice, but she wasn't totally sure at this point. *Minecraft* did allow her to weave together a bit of architecture and some information on water displacement planned for later in the year for science.

She faced an extreme dilemma however. Which *Minecraft* should she use? The one the kids played with was great, but involved shooting zombie sheep and pigs; the Edu version was a bit more sanitized, but had two disadvantages—first, kids couldn't use the mods they'd built on their own or use their previous game play; and second, it undermined some of what she thought might be turning boys off school—the sanitized nature of zero tolerance policies and banning of anything remotely violent.

After the earlier debacle, though, with the parents and administration already looking over her shoulder in regards to her use of games, she decided on the *Minecraft* Edu mod to be used in her classroom mostly to be on the safe side.

Having already made the media decision (*media part 1*), she realized that she was a bit out of synch with the ID4T process, and backed up to specific learning goals and objectives. She realized that *Minecraft* could be used in several different goals at the same time, and that a project-based approach would make sense, what she used to call "units." She decided on a *Minecraft* unit and aligned several learning objectives from math, language arts, science, and reading (*goals and objectives*). The test items were already specified from the standardized test for those standards, so that portion was relatively easy (*testing*). Each of these units had to be properly fleshed out then with careful attention to the learner prerequisites. She was able to do a single survey to determine issues of access and preparedness to use the technology, and then she did separate assessments on the content-specific levels of knowledge of things like water displacement, physics, math concepts, language abilities for the writing assignment she had thought of and aligned with the goals (*learner analysis*).

Mrs. Robinson then turned to texts. She had materials already prepared from previous years, but with the integration of the game, she wasn't sure if her usual texts would work. She examined each one individually and found that three of the five worked with the plans she had with *MinecraftEdu* but she selected two different texts as well that seemed to fit better with her goals as she understood them within this frame (*text selection*). She also identified three non-fiction texts on *Minecraft* that she thought would likely be helpful to her students who were not familiar with *Minecraft* and added them judiciously into the unit plans.

She then turned her attention to the activities and more clear examination of the media selection. She knew the way she wanted to integrate the game into her learning objectives, and had enough familiarity to have a clear idea of how this was coming together. She identified specific things to do within *Minecraft* that would help her students reach their learning goals. She wanted them to learn about water displacement through dropping things into water in *Minecraft*; she wanted them to understand volume and area through building various objects with *Minecraft*; and she knew that she could ask the kids to write to each other within *Minecraft* as part of her language arts development, with a specific focus on proper spelling as much as possible and expression more specifically. She knew the kids would have to read, respond and write throughout that part of the unit. She thought about how to structure the activities and built her lessons. She turned to a more complete media examination and looked carefully at the affordances that *Minecraft* offered. She considered alternatives, but only briefly as this decision was largely made earlier—the real point of this exercise was to try to determine how best to use the game within the overall unit plan (*activities and media*).

She turned her attention to the implementation plans and realized immediately that she had to have *lots* of support to make this work. She had already had one round with other stakeholders that might have shut down the unit because of the use of games, and felt pretty confident with the use of *MinecraftEdu* rather than the commercial off-the-shelf *Minecraft*, but still knew she had lots of communications to work through with parents, administrators and parents. She even connected with school board members and the press to see if they would do a story on the unit once things were moving along a bit more. She worked through a thorough and complete implementation plan, realizing that in this case it was vitally important and figured out what kind of "Plan B" and "Plan C" she might need to get through the unit if things changed in terms of support over time (*implementation*). Mrs. Robinson was pleased overall with the progress of the plan and was excited to begin trying things out.

Mrs. Robinson decided that she would try the new unit and its lessons with the entire class rather than doing small group or individual trials. She informally walked through some *Minecraft* experiences with the kids prior to full trial and was able to see how they interacted with things like writing to each other, reading texts related to *Minecraft*, and ways that they learned about math and science from their work on *Minecraft*. It gave her some informal insights, but didn't quite prepare her for the first full trial. The implementation was exciting and went well overall, but it was full of unexpected derailments, and it took a good deal of energy and work to get the unit off the ground and to keep the kids focused within the game. She did find that there was a great deal of connection between her and the learners, and that they were engaging in an experience that seemed to re-engage the learners in ways that also allowed her to be a caring teacher. She learned from the students, and helped them learn from the game and coached them on the translation from the game to their learning. She conducted both formative and summative evaluations through surveys, tests and observations. She talked to the kids a great deal and learned that there were many ways the lessons could be improved (*formative evaluation*) and after the unit was complete there were rave reviews from all involved. It was clear that there was a good unifying principle underlying the use of *Minecraft* for all the goals except the reading. It was insufficient for the learners to simply read and respond. There was plenty of opportunity within that exchange for good dialogue and further examination of spelling, but there really wasn't a good way to explore other important reading themes at 2nd grade Common Core levels, so summatively she decided that she would have to pull the reading out, and decided instead to use the *Minecraft* texts to help her deal with non-fiction reading activities. (*summative evaluation*). She felt very pleased with the overall success of the unit and the way it had worked for the kids.

**What You Can Do Now (Chapter Summary)**

At this point you will probably be able to:

- Identify the pros and cons of using games in your classroom.
- List the kinds of special considerations you must make in ID4T processes if you employ games in your classroom.
- Identify likely political obstacles to using games in your classroom.
- Tailor your ID4T design to fit a gaming classroom.

# 11

# WHAT ARE THE PRIMARY ADVANTAGES AND DRAWBACKS OF THE ID4T MODEL FOR TEACHERS?

## Chapter Questions

1. What are the most compelling objections to the use of ID4T in your opinion? Why are they?
2. What are the least compelling objections—ones that really have no excuse in your view? Why are they?
3. What are the most compelling motivating forces in your opinion? Why are they?
4. What are the least compelling motivating forces in your opinion? Why are they?

Before you start this chapter, please note that the materials here are most relevant to those of you who are practicing teachers. If you're still a pre-service teacher, you might not find this chapter all that useful, except as it might be able to help you anticipate some of the likely experiences of applying the ID4T model. Be aware, though, that this may also serve to put you off ID4T before you even really try it out. Don't let this be the case. So, proceed with caution if you are a pre-service teacher.

The ID for Teachers (ID4T) model is very flexible as we've seen; it can fit into almost any sort of classroom experience from the use of gaming for learning to the application of open learning concepts. This model can be helpful in making sure that good educational design is happening throughout the creation process. It is not a model that is limited to just one sort of learning or instruction, but rather can be adapted and adopted to a wide variety of settings, learners, theories, and so on. It is exciting to have such a powerful and flexible tool in your own hands now, and by this time in your own evolution as an instructional designer you may be thinking that it all *sounds* pretty good, but even with the earlier case illustrations, it's hard to know whether this will really work for you. *Let's talk about some of the most common concerns, both for and against the use of the ID4T model:*

## Objections

### *This Is Far Too Time Consuming*

At first, learning a new model *will* take time and it may feel like it's just too time-consuming to work at all, but if you give it a chance and, most of all, if you can focus on the heuristics, this model will be a very powerful planning tool that can improve your classroom instruction dramatically.

### *It's Simply Not Feasible*

This is usually related to the time-consuming objection. The reality is that it's not any more expensive and in many cases it will save money because you won't need high-tech media just to use it, but rather only when it's powerfully aligned with your learning goals and objectives. Feasibility is about time and money and, where money is concerned, the ID4T model really doesn't cost more, so it's about it being time consuming. This is a significant hump that simply has to be gotten past in order to hope for significant improvement in classroom practice.

### *My Administration Won't Allow This*

This *could* be a real concern; some administrators have very specific planning processes and ways that they would like to see lesson planning recorded for observations and such. Where this is the case, ID4T can easily fit into the required record keeping with mimimal additional effort. Since I hate to see redundant work in the lives of teachers, it might be worth trying to see if your administration would accept the ID4T model as a malleable yet functional structure for your planning documents. You may learn a great deal about why your administrator wishes to see your planning documents in a particular format and what they'll accept within a range of possibilities. You may also learn about the pressures they have from the district, state, federal government, and even parent or community groups.

*My Learners Are Different and So It Won't Work for Me*

The ID4T model is meant to work with a diversity of learners in a variety of settings throughout the K-12 setting. Even when working in a situation with special needs learners or a wide diversity of racial or socio-economic backgrounds, the ID4T model will still be helpful in thinking through the planning process for your instruction. It is hard to imagine a setting in which the model is truly challenged by the diversity of learners. Paying close attention to the prerequisites and learner characteristics, this model addresses diversity head on.

*Parents Will Object*

Generally, parents may not know what model you're using in your classroom, but it's also possible that parents may not understand the

Photo by Jules Carr-Chellman.

ID4T approach initially, and they may share some concerns, particularly if there's any sense that the time spent in planning is time lost in the classroom with their child. However, for the most part the ID4T model is learned and internalized well if you focus on the common errors and heuristics for the model and therefore again time will not be wasted. The effect is really quite the opposite. Improvements in the classroom follow when the ID4T model is employed. Teachers who have used the model find that while the early stages are time consuming, the end product often yields better instructional planning results.

### It's Too Expensive

This is related to the feasibility and time issues as well. The expense of the ID4T model is really in the additional time that has to be spent in learning to use the model and in more planning time. The only other expenses can be getting texts for examination, or possibly some increases in media use, although as pointed out earlier, the efficiencies gained by proper alignment and media assignment usually outweigh the costs.

### I Doubt It Will Work for Me

Well, this is really a confidence issue. As you work with the model it will feel more and more like a comfortable old shirt you put on. Yes, there's a little effort to the buttons, but it fits beautifully. Confidence is best gained through repeated use of the model, giving particular attention to common errors and heuristics. Increased sensitivity and reference to the errors and heuristics serve as important ways to help you feel the model is simple enough to use even without lots of on-paper planning.

### I'll Lose All Teachable Moments

This is a very important and common concern. Because the model does ask you (or you and your learners in some cases) to create a goal and clear objectives at the outset, the concern here is that the moment-to-moment classroom happenings can't be accounted for even if you wanted them to be. The great moment where a child brings in their favorite book to read to the class could be missed if strict adherence is given to any planning model. It is important to understand that this model isn't meant to be a narrow path that has only one way. It is meant to be a road that may have some minor useful detours that allow us to return to the main path. The notion of planning using this model, or almost any other strong model of instructional design, will, I believe, actually give you *more* rather than less freedom in the classroom. If you know precisely what goals and objectives you're heading for, and you know how they'll be tested, what their activities are, and so forth, you're in a much more confident and capable place. You can take the time to enjoy the teachable moment knowing for sure that you can get on with the planned activities in 15 minutes or the next day or the next week if you need it. And it will all be right there ready for you when you return to it. Do not use this or any other planning model as an excuse for missing those moments—grab them and engage them fully.

## Motivating Forces

### More Effective Learning

The care and time you take to prepare your lessons using the ID4T model can lead to significantly better learning and preparation in the classroom. Simply ensuring that the learners know what is expected of them can dramatically improve learning. There is a great deal of research showing that instructional design models and their various components will tend to increase student enjoyment, student achievement, and classroom organization. However, research also shows that the ID process is rarely used in the classroom. I believe that this is in part because the ID models to this point haven't really focused on easy-to-understand and applicable heuristics, and so I hope this model will be a powerful combination of a clear ID model for use in classrooms and one that will produce stronger, effective learning results.

*More Organized Approach*

Without a doubt the ID4T process creates a more organized approach. With its focus on alignment, this model will help to ensure that the most important milestones in any instructional design process are met. Having the materials organized in this way is very sensible in terms of chronology and will help to bring order to the planning process as well as the resulting documents.

*Increases Alignment among Learning Components*

This is among the most important and significant of contributions that the ID4T (and any ID process for that matter) offers to you as a classroom teacher. Alignment between goals, objectives, tests, activities, media, and so forth, is critical. Focusing on the alignment will help ensure that the learner really is getting to the final goal with all the best aids possible.

*Flexible for Use in Different Classrooms*

As mentioned earlier, this model can be useful in constructivist classrooms, or user-design classrooms. It can be adapted easily to aid in reaching mandated standards-based instruction. It can be useful with a diversity of populations and types of schools. This is a very flexible tool that can be used and adapted to work in almost all learning situations even extending beyond the K-12 environment—although more analysis is needed in any sort of corporate training or higher education. The basics of this model are useful in such a wide variety of settings and this is one of its clear strengths.

*Accounts for Learner Diversity*

By specifically focusing on student prerequisites and learner characteristics as a specific step, this model, like most ID models, specifically attends to issues of learner diversity, which is critical in an increasingly diverse world. As we move into global communities and as we see global connections being made more and more inside our classrooms, this sort of model will be an invaluable tool for making connections across cultures and within cultures.

**What You Can Do Now (Chapter Summary)**

At this point you will probably be able to:

- Discuss the obstacles or objections and the motivating forces in using the ID4T model.
- List those obstacles you're likely to face and some ideas for overcoming them.
- List those motivating forces that are most likely to be at play in your own classroom and how you can maximize those.

# References

Buttram, J. L., & Waters, J. T. (1997). Improving America's schools through standards-based education. National Association of Secondary School Principals, *NASSP Bulletin, 81*(590), 1–6.

Carr, A. A. (1996). Distinguishing systemic from systematic. *Tech Trends, 41*(1), 16–20.

Carr-Chellman, A. A. (2006). *User-design.* Philadelphia, PA, and Mahwah, NJ: Lawrence Erlbaum.

Cavanaugh, C. & Blomeyer, R., (2007). *What works in K-12 online learning.* International Society for Technology in Education.

Committee on Developments in the Science of Learning (2000). *How people learn: Brain, mind experience and school.* Washington, DC: National Academy Press.

Csíkszentmihályi, M. (1996). *Creativity: Flow and the psychology of discovery and invention.* New York: Harper Perennial.

Curry, C., Cohen, L., & Lightbody, N. (2006). Universal design in science learning: An overview of how universal design and technology can advance science for all. *The Science Teacher,* March.

Dick, W., Carey, L. M., & Carey, J. O. (2009). *The systematic design of instruction* (7th ed.). Upper Saddle River, NJ: Merrill.

Duffy, T. M., & Jonassen, D. H. (1991). Constructivism: New implications for instructional technology? *Educational Technology,* May, 7–12.

Ertmer, P. A., & Newby, T. J. (2008). Behaviorism, cognitivism, constructivism: Comparing critical features from an instructional design perspective. *Performance Improvement Quarterly, 6*(4), 50–72.

Frankenberg, E., Seigel-Hawley, G., & Wang, J. (2011). Choice without equity: Charter schools and segregation. *Education Policy Analysis 19*(1).

Gagne, R. M. (1965). *The conditions of learning.* New York: Holt, Rinehart, and Winston.

Hopkins, G. (2004). Is ability grouping the way to go? Or should it go away? *Education World.* Downloaded November 11, 2009, from www.educationworld.com/a_issues/issues002.shtml.

Jonassen, D. H. (1996). *Computers in the classroom: Mindtools for critical thinking.* Englewood Cliffs, NJ: Merrill/Prentice Hall.

Kohn, A. (2001). Beware of the standards, not just the tests. *Education Week, 21*(4), 5.

Krajcik, J., McNeill, K. L., & Reiser, B. (2007). Learning-goal-driven design model: Developing curriculum materials that align with national standards and incorporate project-based pedagogy. *Science Education, 10,* 1–32.

Leshin, C. B., Pollock, J., & Reigeluth, C. M. (1992). *Instructional design strategies and tactics.* Englewood Cliffs, NJ: Educational Technology Publications.

Lofty, J. S. (2003). Standards and the politics of time and teacher professionalisms. *English Education, 35*(3), 195–222.

Madhumita, A., & Kumar, K. L. (1995). Twenty-one guidelines for effective instructional design. *Educational Technology, 35*(May–June), 58–61.

Mager, R. (1975). *Preparing instructional objectives* (2nd ed.). Belmont, CA: Lake Publishing Co.

Marshall, J., Horton, R., & White, C. (2009). Equipping teachers: A protocol to guide and improve inquiry-based instruction. *The Science Teacher.* Downloaded April 13, 2010, from www.britannica.com/bps/additional content/18/37601252/equipping-Teachers.

Merrill, M. D. (1991). Constructivism and instructional design. *Educational Technology,* May, 45–53.

Nitko, A. J. (2004). *Educational assessment of students* (4th ed.). Upper Saddle River, NJ: Merrill/Prentice Hall.

Ravitch, D. (1995). *National standards in American education: A citizen's guide.* Washington, DC: Brookings Institution.

Reiser, R., & Dick, W. (1996). *Instructional planning: A guide for teachers* (2nd ed.). Upper Saddle River, NJ: Allyn & Bacon.

Roblyer, M. D. (1996). The constructivist/objectivist debate: Implications for instructional technology research. *Learning and Leading with Technology, 24,* October, 12–16.

Romiszowski, A. J. (1981). *Designing instructional systems.* New York: Routledge.

Root-Bernstein, R., & Root-Bernstein, M. (1999). *Sparks of genius: The 13 thinking tools of the world's most creative people.* Boston: Houghton Mifflin.

Rossett, A. (1987). *Training needs assessment.* Englewood, NJ: Educational Technology Publications.

Saettler, P. (1990). *The evolution of American educational technology.* Englewood, CO: Libraries Unlimited, Inc.

Satchwell, R. E., & Loepp, F. L. (2002). Designing and implementing an integrated mathematics, science, and technology curriculum for the middle school. *Journal of Industrial Teacher Education, 39*(3), 41–66.

Schuman, L. (1996). Perspectives on instruction. [Online]. Downloaded November 11, 2009, from http://edweb.sdsu.edu/courses/edtec540/Perspectives/Perspectives.html.

Seels, B., & Glasgow, Z. (1998). *Making instructional design decisions* (2nd ed.). Upper Saddle River, NJ: Merrill.

Shen, J., Poppink, S., Cui, Y., & Fan, G. (2007). Lesson planning: A practice of professional responsibility and development. *Educational Horizons, I*(Summer), 248–258.

Skinner, B. F. (1948). *Walden two.* New York: Macmillan.

Skinner, B. F. (1971). *Beyond freedom and dignity.* New York: Knopf.

Vygotsky, L. S. (1978). *Mind and society: The development of higher psychological processes*. Cambridge, MA: Harvard University Press.

Wheelock, A. (1992). *Crossing the tracks: How "untracking" can save America's schools*. New York: New Press.

Wilson, T. A. (1996). *Reaching for a better standard: English school inspection and the dilemma of accountability in American public schools*. New York: Teachers College Press.

# Subject Index